Listening for God
in Everyday Life

Listening for
GOD
IN EVERYDAY LIFE

Joseph D. White, Ph.D.

Our Sunday Visitor
Huntington, Indiana

Copyright © 2020 by Joseph D. White

25 24 23 22 21 20   1 2 3 4 5 6 7 8 9

Our Sunday Visitor Publishing Division
Our Sunday Visitor, Inc.
200 Noll Plaza
Huntington, IN 46750
1-800-348-2440

ISBN: 978-1-68192-350-5 (Inventory No. T2035)
1. RELIGION—Christian Living—Prayer. 2. RELIGION—Christian Living—Spiritual Growth. 3. RELIGION—Christianity—Catholic.
eISBN: 978-1-68192-351-2
LCCN: 2019953225

Cover design: Amanda Falk
Cover art: Shutterstock
Interior design: Amanda Falk

PRINTED IN THE UNITED STATES OF AMERICA

To my wife, Ana — God speaks to me in so many ways through our marriage. I'm so blessed by your love and friendship, and so happy to have you as my partner on this great adventure.

And to our nieces, nephews, and godchildren — The God who made everything you see and everyone you love knows you better than you know yourself, and he deeply desires to be your friend. He is speaking to you. Listen to him, and he will lead you to what your heart longs for.

Contents

Introduction

How Does God Speak to Us Today?

The Jardin des Tuileries, or Tuileries Garden, is the beautiful landscape that surrounds the Tuileries Palace in central Paris. The orange grove of the garden houses the Musée de l'Orangerie, famous for its giant tableaux of Monet's *Water Lilies*. Beneath the trees around the museum are walking paths of fine gravel, perfect for a shady stroll on a bright summer day. We were resting under the trees one day, waiting for the museum to open, when I saw a boy who was about ten years old walking a dog. Or rather, I should say, the dog was walking the boy. The boy had the end of the leash, but the big black dog, excited to be out on the town, was pulling ahead, and the boy was struggling to keep hold of the leash and catch up. As the boy tried to hold his ground, his feet slid on the fine gravel. Finally, losing patience, the boy ran around in front of the dog and looked him in the eye. "Tu ne peux pas nous conduire," he told the dog, "Tu ne sais pas où nous allons!" (You can't lead us; you don't know where we're going!)

Sometimes I wonder if God wants to say the same thing to us. Even though we pray "your will be done" each time we say the Our Father, we can easily fall into a one-way conversation with God that is really about asking him to do our will. Our prayers become never-ending shopping lists of things we'd like to see work out our way. It's important for us to step back and realize that sometimes we don't know what to ask God for. We can't lead ourselves because we don't know where we are going.

Does God speak to us today? Some people doubt it. I'll admit to being skeptical at times when I hear people say, "God put it on my heart that ..." or "God told me ...," especially when they are claiming God told them something that doesn't at all sound as though it would come from God. We surely can fool ourselves into thinking that what is really our will is also God's will. We can look for signs that validate our own plans or perspectives and mistakenly believe God has spoken. History is replete with individuals and groups who did things that were downright *ungodly* "in God's name."

Still, our Judeo-Christian tradition includes many examples of people of faith being led in very tangible ways by a Father who was only waiting for them to say, "Speak, for your servant is listening" (1 Sm 3:10). Sometimes God leads people in ways that are profound and direct, such as in the case of Moses, to whom God spoke through a burning bush. Other times, people of faith experience God's presence in mundane routines like their daily work, as did Saint Thérèse of Lisieux. Others see God at work in small signs — serendipitous happenings, strange coincidences, or words that come through others in their lives.

If our heroes of faith learned to listen to the voice of God, why shouldn't we? Isn't each one of us called to be a saint? While we do indeed have to be careful to not merely seek divine confirmation of what we already want or think, I believe that God does speak to us, perhaps not so much in the way he spoke to prophets long ago, but in everyday ways that we can learn to recognize. He is still a Father, and we are his children. God profoundly respects our free will, so he doesn't impose himself on us, but when we ask him to show us his will, he answers.

In popular culture today, many voices compete for our attention. The hectic pace of everyday life, ubiquitous commercial messages, and multimedia platforms can bring so much noise to our lives that we can forget that God is present. But in the midst of this chaos, a still small voice whispers, "I AM." God is trying to get our attention every day. We just have to learn the language he speaks — it's not always what we might expect. God often speaks through words, but not always. Sometimes we hear him in a sudden inspiration, a feeling of reassurance, a sense of his presence, a renewal of hope, or a call to action. All these experiences of God — whether overt and clear or more silent and subtle — can be examples of God speaking to us.

This book is about listening to God. It's about discovering the various ways he is speaking to us, teaching us, and leading us in our daily lives. We hear God in people who are in need. He speaks to us through other cultures; in the beauty and complexity of creation; in the arts; through friends, family, and children; in the talents and gifts we are given; through humor; in the liturgy; in silence; through the saints; in the midst of struggle; and, of course, in Scripture and Sacred Tradition. Let's embark together on a reflective journey to examine how we can listen for the voice of God and so let our hearts be led by the One who knows us better than we know ourselves.

"Whoever has ears ought to hear" (Mt 11:15).

Chapter 1
God Speaks to Us in Creation

As we boarded the long dugout canoe paddled by two tribes-men with painted bodies dressed in loincloths, I couldn't help but think, "We could disappear out here, and no one would ever know what happened to us."

It was a hot July day in 2007. Our journey had begun with a search for a new and exotic vacation destination. I had read that hunter-gatherer tribes, though rare in the modern world, have almost no incidence of the psychological issues so common to our culture, such as anxiety, depression, and ADHD. As a clinical psychologist, I was eager to find out whether this was true and what made these cultures so impervious to mental illness. So I looked up hunter-gatherer communities still in existence. Many of them are inaccessible to outsiders; they live under the protection of governments and NGOs, who have seen the destruction of indigenous peoples and their cultures by disease, deforestation, and forced assimilation. But in a couple of places around the world, it was still possible to see people living as they had for thousands of years. The Chagres River region of Panama was one of those places.

My wife, Ana, was game for this new adventure, so we bought plane tickets to Panama City and hired a guide to take us into the forest. After the signs of city life faded behind us, we traveled bumpy roads through a mountainous area for about two hours. Shortly after we entered the thick rain forest, we came to the end of the road. "From here," said the guide, "you will have to travel by river." We walked down the muddy embankment, mosquitos buzzing in our ears and biting at our arms and legs, and met Emberá people for the first time. The two tribesmen stood next to a canoe that was clearly hand carved from one of the massive rain forest trees. Our guide said a few words to them and then turned to us, saying, "This is where I leave you. They will take you the rest of the way. I'll pick you up here in two days." I didn't remember this being part of the bargain, but we had come this far, so we nervously stepped into the canoe and began the journey up the river.

The trees surrounding the river were some of the thickest and tallest I had ever seen. It almost seemed as if we were traveling through a tunnel as the river snaked its way through the forest. Pushing aside my fear, I began to take in the colors — greens of all hues, light and dark, yellow sunlight peeking through the thinner canopy of leaves on the tops of the trees, and finally little flashes of brilliant blue. I could hardly believe my eyes, but sure enough, there were blue morpho butterflies all around us. It felt as though they were welcoming us into this new world. Anxiety gave way to excitement, and suddenly we felt at home.

We landed on the shore below the village about an hour later. Some of the children playing on the riverbank had heard the approaching canoe and spread the word through the village that visitors were coming. We were thus greeted by men, women, and children gathered on the shore, dressed in tribal clothing and playing music with reed flutes and animal-skin drums. The children took our hands, and we walked up steep stone steps to the village, which consisted of about twenty-five open-sided, thatched-roof huts fashioned from palm trees and set in a circle with a group meeting area in the center. We set up camp with our "bug hut" mini tents under a larger thatched roof that functioned as a common meeting area for the tribe. They were curious about, and amused by, the supplies we brought, especially the small tents, which they called "little houses." Since they generally slept in the open air, they wondered why we needed those. After all, we already had a roof over our heads. However, since the hut had no walls, we were not about to take our chances with whatever bugs and other creatures we might encounter in the rain forest in the middle of the night. I was sure there would be critters that we had never seen before, and even the familiar bugs would almost certainly be much bigger!

Thankfully, many of the Emberá, who speak their own language, also knew some Spanish, which allowed us to communicate reasonably well. We learned many things in the course of that first weekend visit, but one conversation stands out. Since this particular Emberá community had very limited contact with the outside world (their presence in the Chagres had only been discovered fifteen or twenty years earlier), we wanted to know if they believed in God. We asked where they thought the world came from.

A villager named Andrea, who was second-in-command of the tribe (and the first Emberá woman to have held such a position of authority) responded to this question. She said, "We believe there is a God who made everything because … well, look around. We have trees with fruit to eat and spring water to drink. We have fish to cook and trees to build our homes. There must be a God because look how he has given us everything we need." Andrea's words reminded me of the words of Saint Paul in Romans: "For what can be known about God is evident to them, because God made it evident to them. Ever since the creation of the world, his invisible attributes of eternal power and divinity have been able to be understood and perceived in what he has made" (Rom 1:19–20). Here was an embodiment of these very verses. These people knew God from the things he created. They could see his care for them in the plants, trees, animals, and water he provided.

In his Sermon on the Mount, Jesus also points to various aspects of creation to teach us about the Father. He asks his listeners to "look at the birds in the sky," pointing out that "they do not sow or reap, they gather nothing into barns, yet your heavenly Father feeds them" (Mt 6:26). Jesus then asks his listeners if they aren't more important than those birds. Later, he admonishes his followers to "learn from the way the wild flowers grow" (Mt 6:28), and says, "If God so clothes the grass of the field, which grows today and is thrown into the oven tomorrow, will he not much more provide for you?" (Mt 6: 30). In other stories from the Gospels, Jesus cites other illustrations from nature — the vine and the branches, the fig tree, sheep and their relationship with the shepherd, seeds and how they grow. We sometimes think of these as metaphors, examples Jesus found in nature to explain the things of God. What if it's the other way around? What if God created these things to teach us who he is?

Years before our initial encounter with the Emberá, I was working as a staff psychologist in an acute care psychiatric hospital and residential treatment center for children and teens with serious psychological issues. Most of the four- to sixteen-year-olds at this facility were suffering from post-traumatic stress disorder as the result of severe abuse and neglect. Early in my time at this facility, I noticed a certain species of small bird that built nests all over our campus, some of them low to the ground on ledges, awnings, and windowsills. This placed the birds in close proximity to the sometimes rambunctious children at our center, so we had to be vigilant to make sure the curious kids looked but didn't touch when approaching the birds. I wondered why the birds would make themselves so vulnerable. The birds seemed curious about the kids as well. When a child stopped to look at a nest, usually occupied by the mother bird and her young, the birds would lean toward the kids, looking intently but appearing unafraid. I wondered what these little birds were that seemed so calm in the face of danger. I got my answer when the on-site school for the children in our care started a study of the birds called the "Brown House Sparrow Project." These were sparrows — the same little birds Jesus points to as illustrations of God's care for us: "Are not two sparrows sold for a small coin? Yet not one of them falls to the ground without your Father's knowledge. ... So do not be afraid; you are worth more than many sparrows" (Mt 10:29, 31).

Maybe the sparrows were there in such a visible way to remind these children, who had had such terrible experiences in their short lives, that God had not forgotten them. I started pointing the sparrows out as I walked with children to and from therapy sessions. "That's the bird that built a nest in my windowsill," said one suicidal teen. "That's the bird that landed on my hand," said an eleven-year-old girl who had faced unspeakable abuse in her own home. One child, a six-year-old named Elena,* had been sorely neglected in her early years. Her mother was an addict who supported her drug habit through prostitution, and she often left young Elena home alone, sometimes without food, to fend for herself. Elena and I spent much time watching the birds, particularly the mother's interactions with her babies, talking about how the mother cared for them and brought them the food they needed. Elena needed to see that there was a different way from what

---

* Name has been changed.

she had experienced. If she was to be successful in a new home after treatment, she would have to allow for the possibility that she could trust someone to take care of her. So God taught her this lesson through the birds he made.

I left my work at that center later that year to start a new family counseling program in our diocese. During my last weeks, I talked with each of my patients, preparing them for the transition to a new therapist. When I told Elena about my impending departure, she looked at me with big brown eyes and furrowed eyebrows and said, "But you can't leave. You take care of me, like the mother bird and the baby birds." My heart just about broke.

On the day I left, Elena gave me a crayon picture she had drawn as a goodbye present. In the buzz of activity on my last day, I received other pictures and notes from the kids and never had an opportunity to talk to Elena about what she had drawn. On first glance, I couldn't make out what it was. Weeks later, unpacking my things in my new office at the diocese, I framed Elena's drawing and hung it on my wall. As I admired it, I was able to make out what she had drawn — a mother bird in a nest with three babies. I keep that picture as a reminder of how God speaks to us of his great love for us through the things he has made.

LISTENING FOR GOD IN HIS CREATION

Reflect for a moment on experiences in which you have been filled with wonder and awe at God's creation.

What image of nature from Sacred Scripture stands out to you? Why?

Go for a walk in a nearby park (or on an adventure at a natural attraction such as a mountain, waterfall, or canyon). Ask God to help you discover him in your experience of his creation.

Chapter 2
God Speaks to Us through People in Need

My friend Kevin told me a story from when he was working in an office job in Manhattan. On his lunch break, he would attend daily Mass, then buy a lunch to go and eat it back at his desk as he worked. One day when Kevin left the church after Mass, he encountered a man who was obviously homeless. He looked hungry. When Kevin stopped by a fast-food stand to order his lunch, he asked for a burger, fries, and soda. Then, remembering the man he had seen, he said, "You know what? Make that two of everything." He asked that the two combos be placed in separate bags and then took one of the bags to the homeless man, who was still standing outside the church. The man gratefully received the food. As Kevin turned around and began to walk away, he heard the man call after him, "Thanks for taking care of me, Kevin." Kevin stopped in his tracks; he hadn't told the man his name. How did this man know who he was? He quickly turned back around, but the man to whom he had brought lunch was nowhere in sight.

Was this a heavenly encounter? Perhaps. Either way, it serves to remind us that Jesus is really and truly present in people in need. After all, Jesus tells us in Matthew 25:40, "Whatever you did for one of these least brothers of mine, you did for me."

For several years, my wife, her parents, and I made an annual trip over Labor Day weekend to take clothing and catechetical supplies to an impoverished community on the Mexican side of the United States–Mexico border. The weather was usually quite warm, but one year it was brutal. After coming across the border on foot, we had spent all day outside in the streets of the small border town, and the sun was beating down. In our last few hours, we spent what was left of our pocket change on bottled water. By the time we decided to call it a day, I was down to my last bottle. We noticed an unusually long line as we approached the border crossing to return. This made sense in retrospect, as it was our first visit across the border since the 9/11 terrorist attack the year before; the officials on the U.S. side were carefully scrutinizing those coming across. The line snaked through the town plaza, and as we waited in the sun, children approached the day tourists in line, asking them if they wouldn't like to buy one last trinket or piece of gum. We recognized some of the children — a boy who had approached us earlier, selling handcrafted refrigerator magnets in the shape of turtles with legs that wiggled when you moved them around; a girl who sold packs of five pieces of candy-coated gum wrapped in little squares; a young teen we had seen sweeping the sidewalk and pausing to wipe the sweat from his brow.

The line moved so slowly that I became acutely aware of the sun beating on the top of my head, making it feel like my hair was melting just a little. I took a drink from my bottle of water. Then, realizing that I had only half a bottle left, I decided to save the rest to see me through the long line. Just then, I felt a little tap in the middle of my back. I turned around to see a small girl of about seven or eight years. "¿Señor, por favor, puedo tener el resto de su agua?" she asked, her eyes big and pleading. This girl wanted the rest of my water. I handed it to her without a second thought. (You probably would have done the same.) Most kids I knew wouldn't drink from someone else's bottle of water, let alone a stranger's. But this girl was so thirsty, it made no difference to her.

As we walked across the border several minutes later, I heard an inner voice: "I was thirsty, and you gave me something to drink" (see Mt 25:35). My eyes filled with tears in that moment, for I realized that while I had given only a half a bottle of water, this little girl had given me something much more precious — an encounter with Jesus Christ.

Every time we encounter a person in need, we have an opportunity to recognize the face of Christ. Saint Teresa of Calcutta (Mother Teresa) understood this well: "I see Jesus in every human being," she once said. "I say to myself, this is hungry Jesus, I must feed him. This is sick Jesus. This one has leprosy or gangrene; I must wash him and tend to him. I serve because I love Jesus."

To serve Jesus, we have to see Jesus. As difficult as it might be sometimes to see people in need, we must be determined not to look away. In 2010, I was reading the news online and came across an article about a rehabilitation center in Cambodia — the first of its kind — for young children who had been rescued from sex trafficking. This was before that type of exploitation was well known to the general public. The article focused on a six-year-old girl who had been through a harrowing experience and was showing classic symptoms of post-traumatic stress disorder.

The director of the center, who was herself a survivor of sex trafficking, said, "There are no child psychologists in Cambodia. We don't always understand the behaviors we see in these children or how to help them." It occurred to me that my experience as a child psychologist treating children who were abuse survivors might give me something to offer to this work.

A few weeks later, I heard that John and Kathy Tucker, missionaries from our diocese who were working in Cambodia, were visiting the United States and would be stopping by the diocesan pastoral center where I worked. I made it a point to meet them and ask them if a white man from the United States would be able to offer any help to the care workers who worked with child victims of trafficking there. I knew I would not be able to stay in Cambodia long enough to work with the children myself, but perhaps I could do some trainings for the people who cared for them on a daily basis, teaching them to recognize and understand symptoms of trauma in children and to create a therapeutic environment in which they could heal. John leaned over my desk, looked me straight in the eye, and asked, "Can you come tomorrow?" He reiterated that there were no child psychologists in Cambodia — and in fact very few educated people — since the Khmer Rouge, the oppressive military regime of Pol Pot, had carried out a massive genocide in the late 1970s, killing everyone in the country with any education (amounting to about a third of the country's citizens).

I told them my wife and I would need time to plan and to save up enough funds to go, but that we would like to come and help. Kathy told me, "Joseph, one thing we have learned from working all these years in Cambodia is that if you believe God wants you to do something, you need to decide to do it, and God will provide a way."

"Then we'll do it," I said. By the end of the day, we had secured funding for the trip. Ana and I did some reading and research on Cambodia. We were shocked to find that at that time, there were seven thousand children homeless on the streets of Phnom Penh. This large number of vulnerable kids was one reason child exploitation and trafficking were so prevalent there. Some of these children would sell themselves on the streets at night so they could afford to buy food.

We decided that we wouldn't look away while we were there, no matter what we heard or saw. Most of the time, not looking away wasn't as difficult as we thought it would be. We spent most of our days at New Hope for Cambodian Children, the extraordinary home for children with HIV that John and Kathy founded. We did trainings for the staff on child development and on child behavior management. We also did trainings for two other charities on caring for children who have experienced trauma. On those days, our focus was on teaching skills to the adults who were so eager to learn. But we had free time one day and decided to go to Choeung Ek, the best known of the "killing fields," sites of a large number of the genocidal killings of the Khmer Rouge, and now a memorial to those who had died.

It was hard not to look away from the photos of those who had died, a horrifying monument that contained rows and rows of human skulls, and the descriptions of the atrocities committed there. But children visited us at the fence as we walked around the grounds, granting us some short reprieves from attending to the grim memorial. More street children, perhaps. Apparently, the kids we had encountered had spread the word that Americans were visiting, because a large group of them waited for us at the exit. They began to surround us, and one of the guards at the facility raised a long stick. It looked as though he might use it on some of the kids, so I stepped in the way and said, "No, it's OK." Ana and I talked with the kids and handed out dollar bills from a stack we had brought in case something like this should happen.

Ordinarily, I wouldn't advocate handing out dollar bills to children in the streets of a developing country, but I knew that some of these children were on their own, and fifty cents could buy them dinner. For some of them, this would be a night they didn't have to sell themselves in order to eat. But the crowd of children grew and grew as we handed out the dollar bills. Finally, the driver we had hired to take us around the city grew worried for us and told us it was time to go. I handed out my remaining dollars as we got into the car. Once we were safely inside, one more little face appeared in the window next to me — a girl who hadn't received a dollar bill. I was out of money. I had nothing left to give. She put her hand on the window and looked at me, eyes wide. For me, this was the hardest moment to not look away. I put my hand on the window, opposite hers, looked into her eyes, and said, "I'm sorry." I hope she knew that I cared about her even though I had nothing left to give.

This was a painful experience, but a necessary one. If we want to listen to God in those who are in need, we must be determined not to look away. If we remain present with those who are suffering, we have an opportunity to see the suffering Christ in those who are poor and marginalized, and we hear his call to show them love. In this way, we have an opportunity to be Christ to them as well.

The persons in need that we encounter aren't always strangers. Sometimes they are very close to home. When the above-quoted passage from Matthew 25 comes up in the readings at Sunday Mass, I imagine that some parents of young children hear those words and say to themselves, "We should be doing more for people in need, but I'm just so busy right now with young children. Maybe when the kids get older, we can do a family service project together." Indeed, I hope these parents do find ways to get involved with works of mercy as a family, but I hope they also discover that they are engaging in works of mercy every day in their work as parents. In their wonderful book *The Corporal Works of Mommy (and Daddy Too)*, Dr. Greg and Lisa Popcak relate how their young son pointed out, after hearing Jesus' words in Matthew 25, that Mom and Dad did these things all the time. If you are a parent, how often have you given food to the hungry (three times a day plus snacks)? When have you given drink to the thirsty (even when you weren't sure they were really thirsty, but maybe just trying to get out of bed one more time before going to sleep)? You've clothed the naked. You've cared for the sick (you've probably even had the sick get sick on you). You've even visited the imprisoned (what about those talks you have when the kids are in time out?).

Why is it so important to recognize these labors as works of mercy? Because in every work of mercy, every time we encounter someone in need, we have an opportunity to meet Jesus. We definitely want to see Jesus in our families, but sometimes this is a challenge. Mother Teresa said, "It is easy to love the people far away. It is not always easy to love those close to us. It is easier to give a cup of rice to relieve hunger than to relieve the loneliness and pain of someone unloved in our own home. Bring love into your home, for this is where our love for each other must start."*

Jesus calls to us today in those who are in need. He reminds us that we are his Body. He commands us to listen to those who need us to accompany them in their struggle, to raise our voices against injustice, to stretch out our hands to those who need food, to embrace those who are longing for healing. Jesus is speaking to us in the least of those among us. Jesus also meets us in the needs of those closest to us — a friend or family member in need of patience, presence, or an act of love. God is speaking to us. Are we listening to his voice?

---

* David Scott, *A Revolution of Love: The Meaning of Mother Teresa* (Chicago: Loyola Press, 2005), 62.

LISTENING FOR GOD IN PEOPLE IN NEED

When have you encountered people in need? What has God told you about himself in these encounters?

When is it most difficult for you to see Jesus in a person who is in need? Why?

Make a special effort this week to "meet Jesus" in a family member and in a stranger who is in need. Reflect on how seeing Jesus in these individuals changes the experience of giving.

Chapter 3
God Speaks to Us through Children

I was just over halfway through college, and I was feeling directionless. Back home for the summer, I was struggling in my faith, trying to figure out where I would attend graduate school (and when), and working a summer job at a day camp at a local child development center. If my confusion and frustration with life showed on my face, I didn't know it. It was just an ordinary day, and the kids were on the playground. The southwestern sun was scorching everyone, but it was less noticeable to the little people who were moving at the speed of sound. Some of the kids were climbing on the jungle gym, turning upside down, and laughing. Others were playing freeze tag on the blacktop. I wish I could be so carefree, I thought. But I have to worry about how I'm going to be a grown-up.

Then four-year-old Alexandra came up to me and tugged on my arm. A wiry little sprite with long blond hair and a sparkle in her eyes, she smiled at me and said, "Know who will take care of you? God will!"

I was a little taken aback. How did she know? Well ... she didn't, but God did, and God often chooses to speak to us through the humble, the little, "these least ones." The prophet Moses thought God shouldn't have chosen him, because he was a poor speaker. Jesus himself was born a baby in a barn to a poor teenage mother from Nazareth. "Can anything good come from Nazareth?" the people would one day scoff (Jn 1:46). And it was through little Alexandra that God spoke to me on that day.

What she said was true. God did take care of me. A year later in that very spot, I would meet the new prekindergarten teacher, the woman who is the love of my life — my wife, Ana. Two years later, I would go on to graduate school. Three years later, I would discover the Catholic Church. God kept the promise he made through this small child, and I'm glad I paid attention. But knowing how God is fond of speaking in humble, little ways, I wonder how often I have missed his still, small voice. How many other times has he tried to tell me something while I was looking for a more impressive messenger?

A few years later, my wife and I were teaching a special Advent lesson in our Wednesday night First Communion class. This was our last class before Christmas, and we hoped to leave the children with a few new insights about a familiar story. We asked, "Why did God lead both the shepherds and the Magi to the place where Jesus was born?" It was really a rhetorical question — we didn't expect the second graders to have the answer to this one.

Then Emily raised her hand. She was a religious education prodigy, to be sure. Over the course of the semester, she had conveyed insights about God and the Church that belied her seven years. This was made all the more amazing by the fact that Emily had a tumultuous home life. Her mother was a new convert and her father an atheist, and there was much family discord about this and many other issues. Despite her dexterity with theological issues, we didn't expect Emily to get this especially challenging question right, but our curiosity was certainly piqued. "Emily, do you have some ideas about that?" one of us asked.

"Yes," she replied. "God wanted the rich wise men and the poor shepherds to come because Jesus was for everybody, not just people who were rich or important. He especially wanted to tell the people who were poor not to lose hope, because Jesus was coming for them. God's *best* gift was for *everyone*."

We looked at each other, amazed at her response. One of us choked out, "Yes, that's very good. Jesus was for everyone, and God wanted to show it." It was only fitting that God should reveal himself so profoundly in the mind of this little child, just as he first revealed the birth of his Son to humble shepherds so long ago.

In Luke 18:15-17, we read an account of people bringing children to Jesus. Knowing that Jesus was an important teacher and feeling that he did not have time for this sort of thing, the apostles scolded the people. But Jesus invited the children over and told the Apostles, "Let the children come to me and do not prevent them; for the kingdom of God belongs to such as these. Amen, I say to you, whoever does not accept the kingdom of God like a child will not enter it" (vv. 16-17).

The Gospel writer places this passage between two others that may give us clues to its meaning. Jesus has just told a parable in which a Pharisee and a tax collector go to the Temple to pray. The Pharisee congratulates himself by thanking God that he is not like the sinners he sees around him. He talks about his good deeds and his sacrifices. The tax collector acknowledges his own sin and cries out to God for mercy. Jesus states that the tax collector is the one who went home justified before God, adding, "for everyone who exalts himself will be humbled, and the one who humbles himself will be exalted" (Lk 18:14).

Just after the encounter with the children, a rich official approaches Jesus, asking what he needs to do to inherit eternal life. Jesus reminds him of the commandments, and the man claims that he has kept all of them since his youth. Then Jesus says, "There is still one thing left for you: sell all that you have and distribute it to the poor, and you will have a treasure in heaven. Then come, follow me" (v. 22). The man goes away sad, too attached to his wealth to "accept the kingdom of God like a child."

A colleague of mine tells of a child she encountered while working as a parish director of religious education. It was the Easter Vigil, and the child was to be baptized. Because the little girl was six years old, the priest wanted to make sure she knew something about what she was doing. "Do you know what's going to happen?" he asked. "Yes," she replied confidently. "I'm going to become a Catholic," she said. "You're going to pour water on my head and say, 'I baptize you in the name of the Father, and of the Son, and of the Holy Spirit,' and then I'll be Catholic."

"Good enough," said the priest to himself, somewhat impressed.

After her baptism, the little girl was eager to be confirmed. It is very unusual to confirm a child so young, but when the adults attempted to explain this to her, she looked at them pleadingly and said, "But I need the Holy Spirit." Needless to say, she was confirmed. Afterward, she waited eagerly in the line for her first Communion. Her eyes widened as she saw the Host raised before her. After she took the Host into her mouth, she wrapped her arms around her chest and squeezed tight.

"Jesus," she exclaimed. "I've waited so long to hold you in my heart!"

Like the disciples in the Gospel, many adults present that night had thought that perhaps these things of God were too serious, too important, to be approached by a child so small. They wondered if this little girl was old enough to appreciate the Sacraments of Baptism, Confirmation, and Eucharist. To their surprise, *she* taught *them* a lesson about how to appreciate these gifts. "At that time Jesus said in reply, 'I give praise to you, Father, Lord of heaven and earth, for although you have hidden these things from the wise and the learned you have revealed them to the childlike'" (Mt 11:25).

Accepting the kingdom of God like a child means humbling ourselves, putting down our baggage, and trusting that God is more wonderful than anything we could ever do or have. Children are already humble before adults. They are small; they don't have much; they don't know the things we know. They're often even afraid of us when we are strangers to them. They come to us with nothing but themselves, and they trust us to love them anyway.

Are you willing to hear God speak through the voice of a child? Do you believe that he can teach us some of his most important lessons through these least ones? My own work with children and families has made me a believer. God is always near to these little ones, and they have taught me quite a bit. They are smaller than we are, and their voices can be soft. You'll have to be willing to bend down and get close. But if you do, you might hear them whisper, "God will take care of you, too."

LISTENING FOR GOD IN ENCOUNTERS WITH CHILDREN

What has God taught you through your own children, grandchildren, nieces or nephews, or children with whom you have worked?

What would it take for you to become more like a little child — humble and trusting before God the Father?

Spend some time with a child you know. Allow the child to choose the activity or topic of conversation and listen closely. What is God trying to tell you through this encounter?

Chapter 4
God Speaks to Us through Other Cultures

It can be so enriching to travel and to experience other cultures and traditions. Other cultures offer us new perspectives, ideas, and ways of seeing the world. They can also help us to better understand our own culture and our place within it. This has certainly been the experience of my wife and me, especially in our many visits with the Emberá, our indigenous friends in the Panamanian rain forest.

On our first visit with the Emberá, since the particular community we visited was still relatively isolated and had little contact with the outside world, we set out with the idea that we would try not to introduce things from our world into the culture. Fans of the television show *Star Trek* will recognize this principle as the "Prime Directive" — Star Fleet's instruction to space travelers that they should not introduce things into a culture that are unknown to the culture, particularly in the areas of technology or cultural ideals, and thus risk interfering with the natural development of the culture. It turns out that this is easier in theory than in practice.

The Emberá, especially the children, are very curious about what visitors bring; as we unpacked, they looked through our things without reservation. The children found a bag of Twizzlers candy, so we showed them that it was food and offered it to those nearby. After taking one stick each, they ran across the common area of the village to the huts on the other side. When we saw that they were showing the other children there what they had received, I immediately regretted having given the candy to the kids because we wouldn't have enough for the children who would come back with them. To our surprise, however, when the other children came to us, each already had a small piece of Twizzler in hand. We then understood that the children to whom we had given the candy had run over not to show off their treasure but to divide and share it with the other children. We saw this behavior over and over in the village. Everyone made it a priority to share what they had with others, calling to mind the description of the earliest Christian community in Acts 2:44: "All who believed were together and had all things in common."

On the same visit, we took out a beach ball we had brought with us, inflated it, and gave it to the twenty or so kids playing in the common area of the village. (Yes, this was yet another violation of the Prime Directive, but they loved it.) The kids ran and kicked the ball, threw it to one another, and jumped up and hit it with their heads as it bounced over them. When one little boy who was about seven or eight years old jumped quite high and headed the beach ball, his foot came down on a sharp rock that had found its way into the play area. The children were dressed only in loincloths — they had no shoes. Even though this little boy's foot was calloused from walking through the forest, climbing trees, and the like, it was no match for the rock he landed on. He immediately collapsed to the ground, shrieking in pain. Then something remarkable happened. The other children signaled to one another, immediately stopped the ball, then formed a circle around the injured boy until an adult came, helped him up, and carried him away. Even then, they didn't resume playing until the boy was feeling better. They couldn't have fun playing the game if someone was hurting from playing it. If something similar had happened back home, I'm not sure the other children who were playing would have noticed; or if they did, they probably wouldn't have stopped the game, even for a minute. I was struck by the way each Emberá child felt the pain of the child who had been hurt. It reminded me of one of Saint Paul's admonitions to Christians: "Bear one another's burdens, and so you will fulfill the law of Christ" (Gal 6:2).

In his General Audience Address of September 9, 1998, Pope John Paul II, drawing on the writings of the Second Vatican Council, speaks of the "seeds of the Word" that can be seen in other traditions. He makes the case that since all peoples are created by God, they all naturally strive for God, and this striving is inspired by the Holy Spirit. He quotes his first encyclical letter, *Redemptor Hominis*, saying, "There is but a single goal to which is directed the deepest aspiration of the human spirit as expressed in its quest for God … for the full dimension of its humanity, or in other words, for the full meaning of human life" (11). Each culture strives for God in its own way, and while as Catholics we believe that the fullness of truth is found in the Catholic Church, we might find that some cultures with fewer people who take the name "Catholic" or "Christian" may, in some respects, more closely approximate the ideals of our faith than our own culture does. The way the Emberá people valued sharing good things with one another and taking care of those who are suffering inspired us.

We observed another striking difference between Emberá culture and our own. On one of our early visits, a small group of the Emberá men asked us if we were "children of God." We told them that we were Christians and did indeed consider ourselves children of God. They informed us that a Christian missionary from the United States had visited them and told them that God was angry with them because they were not fully clothed from their necks to their ankles. "Why did he say this? Why would God be angry with us because of how we dress?" they wanted to know. We replied that we did not think God was angry with them for their clothing. After all, their clothing was modest according to their own cultural standards and was functional for them. Dressed like Westerners in the rain forest, we found that the heat and high humidity often left us with clothes that were hot, damp, and heavy at the end of the day. Our clothes simply were not practical for them.

However, we told them that he might say this because in the culture he comes from (also our culture), people sometimes objectify the body — viewing another person as a "thing" rather than a person, and that in our culture, some people associate clothing that shows a lot of skin with this objectification of the body. The men appeared absolutely dumbfounded by this. After several seconds of silence, one of the men asked, "How did this happen?" It seemed absolutely preposterous to them that people would be viewed as "things." In a society with no mirrors and no television, where everyone dressed the same way, the human body, and indeed the human person, was viewed so differently that even the young men in the culture struggled to understand how the human body could be objectified.

Our experiences with the Emberá taught me that many of the assumptions we make about human nature — those things that cause us to get cynical and say, "That's just the way people are" — aren't necessarily universals. This realization simultaneously presents a challenge and gives hope: We can be better than we are.

One way we could start "being better" in our Western culture today is by listening more — being present and giving others opportunities to share their perspectives and stories. American culture today is so polarized that nearly everything seems to be associated with a particular political agenda or perspective. This can cause us to be highly suspicious of one another's motives and to stop listening immediately when we get the sense that someone's point of view is different from our own. We are already seeing how this creates a society in which few problems get solved and people resort to name calling instead of dialogue to settle political and, unfortunately, even religious differences.

Contrast this with the Native American tradition of the "talking stick." The Iroquois and other indigenous peoples have used the talking stick to assist in dialogue and understanding between people with different points of view. The stick, usually decorated with feathers and other traditional objects, was held by the person addressing the group. Only the person holding the stick could speak — the others had to listen with attention, even if they had very different points of view. When the person holding the talking stick felt he or she had been heard, that person would then pass the stick to someone else. From a very early age, children in these indigenous communities were taught to listen with attention and understanding to the opinions of others, even if they disagreed. Being present, paying attention, and allowing others to have their say without interruption helped everyone feel heard and helped the group move toward a consensus.

Imagine if we could show this kind of respect for opposing points of view in our own culture. We might learn new things that would change our perspective; at the very least, we could have a deeper understanding for the sincerely held beliefs of others. Perhaps then we would keep sight of the dignity of each person. Perhaps we could finally get to work solving problems if we could focus the discussion on the content of the argument rather than the perceived motives or character flaws of opposing parties. At the very least, a little more listening and a lot less interrupting might help us live in peace with one another despite our differences.

Many factors have contributed to the cultural differences around the world. Let us see the best in people, looking at others with the same mercy God shows when he looks at us. Let us search for the good we can find in each culture and its traditions. Through the diversity of humankind, God might be trying to teach us lessons we desperately need to learn. If we listen with open hearts, we might come away with a new way of seeing the world. And we might even learn more about ourselves.

LISTENING FOR GOD IN OTHER CULTURES

What experiences have you had in cultures that were different from your own? Have you traveled to places very different from home? Have you attended a cultural event hosted by a group with different traditions from yours? What might God be trying to teach you through your experiences?

How have you experienced God's universal truth through the lens of a different culture?

Did you gain any new insights about yourself through experiencing another cultural perspective?

Chapter 5
God Speaks to Us through Family and Relationship

Just over a year ago, I faced the most profound loss of my life thus far: My grandfather died at ninety-five years of age. Grandpa loomed large in the lives of my brothers and sisters and me. He cared for us on a daily basis when we were young, taught us to read and write, took us to the park and played with us, made up stories and poems, helped us discover music, and most importantly taught us the value of faith. I remember countless conversations with Grandpa about Scripture, as well as discussion about the application of faith to daily life. My siblings and I were raised in an active and vibrant church with a dynamic children's ministry and large youth group, but the first place we experienced God was in our family.

God uses the family to teach us several of the most important truths of our faith. The first truth God teaches us through the family is the most foundational of all — that God himself is a *communion of persons.* Genesis 1:27 says:

> God created mankind in his image;
>   in the image of God he created them;
>   male and female he created them.

Scholars like Pope Saint John Paul II have pointed out that this passage suggests not only that we are individually created in the image of God, but also that we are created *male and female* in order to image God in a particular way. Our one God is, in his very essence, a communion of three divine Persons — Father, Son, and Holy Spirit. Humans, in our creation as male and female, are made to be in communion with one another; it is stamped into our very bodies. In the life of the Holy Trinity, the Father gives himself in love to the Son. The Son, in turn, offers his whole self to the Father, and the Spirit of Love between the Father and the Son is a Third Person — the Holy Spirit, who proceeds from the Father and the Son. Likewise, in the marital relationship, when husband and wife give themselves fully to one another in love, holding nothing back, there is the possibility of a third person — a baby. For this reason, the *Catechism of the Catholic Church* tells us that "the Christian family is a communion of persons, a sign and image of the communion of the Father and the Son in the Holy Spirit" (2205).

Interestingly, this portion of the story of creation is the first passage of Scripture in which the text is set like poetry, which typically indicates that it is a song (see Philippians chapter 2 for another example). Ancient Jewish teaching was by oral tradition, with lessons passed on through story and song. The most important points were handed down through song, because melody and rhythm help the words stick in our minds. (I, for one, am a walking encyclopedia of song lyrics from the 1980s. They serve no purpose for me, but the songs of my high school years were catchy enough that I couldn't forget them if I tried.) So the fact that God created human beings in his own image and likeness is the main point of the story of creation.

A second truth God teaches us through the family concerns how he relates to us through Jesus Christ. The fifth chapter of Saint Paul's Letter to the Ephesians is often misunderstood. When this passage comes up in the readings we hear at Mass, it can be interesting to look around and see how people are processing what is said. We have all probably been guilty of getting distracted during the Liturgy of the Word, but everyone always seems to pay attention when they hear the words "Wives should be subordinate to their husbands" (v. 22). You can sometimes see a few husbands jokingly nudge their wives as if to say, "Did you hear that, honey?" You can see other people stiffen up a little, perhaps wondering, "When are they going to update the lectionary?"

However, if all we hear in this passage is that wives should be subordinate, we have completely missed the point Saint Paul is making. The passage begins with the words "Be subordinate to one another out of reverence for Christ" (v. 21). In other translations, "be subordinate" is rendered as "submit yourselves." When we "submit" something, we are giving it to someone else. So Saint Paul is saying that we honor Jesus by giving ourselves to one another. He goes on to give some examples of this. The idea that wives would give themselves to their husbands was axiomatic in Saint Paul's day and culture, as women were considered almost like the property of their husbands. But Saint Paul is about to turn this idea on its head to offer a new picture of marriage in Christ. He goes on to say, "Husbands, love your wives, even as Christ loved the church and handed himself over for her" (v. 25).

Now this idea, fully understood, was new and different: not only are wives to give themselves fully to their husbands, but husbands are called to give themselves to their wives, and not just a little bit: Christ gave himself for us completely — Body, Blood, Soul, and Divinity. Saint Paul leaves no doubt that Christian marriage also means husbands giving themselves totally to their wives. What happens when two people offer themselves as gift to one another? The two become one. As Jesus said, quoting the creation story in Genesis 2:24, "So they are no longer two, but one flesh" (Mt 19:6). Our earthly marriages generally fall short of Jesus' self-gift to the Church, but here God gives us both a vision of what we are striving for and the hope that through the grace of marriage we might learn to become ever more self-giving. This happens in the little moments — letting the other choose the movie on movie night, cleaning up after the other, anticipating one another's needs. In our culture, women still tend to do more of this than men. However, Jesus' self-gift to the Church is not 25 percent or even 50 percent but 100 percent, so we men, especially, have quite a long way to go. Let us pray for the grace to grow in self-giving love.

Saint Paul goes on to call this mutual self-gift a "great mystery" (Eph 5:32). The word he uses in the Greek is *mysterion*, which literally means "a truth whispered." What truth is being whispered here? Saint Paul tells us, "I speak in reference to Christ and the church." Jesus Christ gives himself completely to us — Body, Blood, Soul, and Divinity — and each of us is called to respond to this gift of self by giving ourselves to him in return. By offering ourselves to Jesus Christ, who is all-giving, we do not lose ourselves. Rather we *find* ourselves in him. We become the people God made us to be.

So God uses marriage and family to teach us about his own nature and about how he relates to us through Jesus Christ. A third truth God teaches us through the family concerns our relationship to him and to one another. When Jesus teaches his disciples to pray, he tells them to call God "Father" (in Hebrew,

Abba). Scripture tells us that through baptism, we have all received a spirit of adoption through which we can call God "Abba, Father" (Rom 8:15). I did not fully appreciate the meaning of the word *Abba* until a few years ago when I was visiting Jerusalem. It happened to be *Sukkot*, the Feast of Tabernacles, an ancient Jewish celebration mentioned in the Bible and still celebrated today. Families from all over Israel were visiting Jerusalem. I saw a number of families in traditional dress near the Western Wall — the only part of the Temple complex remaining from Jesus' time. One family walked along with the father several feet ahead. A little boy who was about two reached up with his arms and ran to catch up with his father, calling out, "Abba! Abba!" Only then did I understand that *Abba* is what babies and young children call their fathers. In English, it is probably closer to "Daddy" than to "Father." When Jesus tells the disciples to address the Father as "Abba," he is implying a tender relationship between God and us. He is showing us a God we can run to, lift our arms toward, and ask to carry us.

And if God is our Father, then who are we to one another? We are brothers and sisters. Is this how we think of one another? In a healthy family, sisters and brothers might disagree. They might have different interests and tastes, but they still love one another and gather around the table together for family meals and celebrations. As our society has become increasingly politically polarized, our Church, too, has seen increased polarization. Can we still accept one another as brothers and sisters in Christ? Can we walk with one another, pray for one another, and gently guide one another? There will naturally be disagreements and differences of opinion, some even serious, but healthy families know how to forgive, to be considerate of one another, and to gather again around the table.

But it would be remiss of me, as a child and family psychologist, not to acknowledge that while all of our families fall short of imaging the communion we find in the Blessed Trinity or the complete self-giving love found in Jesus Christ toward the Church, many families suffer profoundly from discord, division, and brokenness.

One summer while I was working as a group leader in a vacation Bible school program for children ages five through eleven, we were discussing things we find challenging to do at home. One of the children described the conflict between himself and his older brother and then went on to explain his relationship with his siblings, half-siblings, and stepsiblings. As he reflected on how much his family had changed and the conflicts and separations between his family members, he quietly commented, "I just realized how messed up my family really is." He looked down at the floor as he said this. My heart broke for this little boy, and I struggled to find something helpful to say in this group setting. After a quick prayer, I said, "Every family is different, and no family is perfect, but God always gives us someone in our lives we can connect with and count on. Can you think of someone in your life who shows you God's love?" He quickly replied, "Yes. My dad," and he smiled a little. Each of the kids then took turns naming someone in their family who shows them God's love.

On another occasion at vacation Bible school, we were talking about "God sightings," times we had an experience of God through something that happened in our day. One little girl said that she had been feeling very sad because she had not seen her father in a long time, and then her little sister grew afraid because of a storm outside, so she held her sister and made her feel better. She said she experienced God in that moment as she realized how lucky she and her sister were to have one another when they couldn't be with others they love.

Some of us may have experienced so much pain in our family of origin that we have difficulty finding God there. Instead, we might experience God in the family he gives us through marriage, neighbors, and friends. In any case, no one is meant to be alone. We need each other. God made us that way, and he speaks to us through family and relationship.

God uses the family to teach us about some of the most important truths of our faith — who God is as a communion of persons, how he relates to us through Jesus Christ, how we approach God as Father, and who we are to one another as sisters and brothers. In all likelihood, these are not simply analogies — devices used by the inspired writers of Scripture to help make the point. No, God's plan for us existed from the beginning, and so we may assume God *created* marriage and family to teach us these truths — to prepare us to live as the family of God.

LISTENING FOR GOD IN FAMILY AND RELATIONSHIP

What have you learned about your faith from your family? Who was an example to you?

How does your family image the communion of the Trinity and the self-giving love between Jesus and the Church?

Despite the imperfections that might be present in your family, who is someone in your family or among your friends who shows you God's love?

Chapter 6
God Speaks to Us in the Liturgy

When I arrived at graduate school, before I became Catholic, I was searching for a spiritual home. Ana, ever the good sport, was along for the ride, but unbeknownst to me, she was feeling a longing to return to the Eucharist. Shortly before we married, I had told her that I could probably be OK in just about any Christian church, but I would never ever be Catholic. Sure that returning to the Church would cause conflict in our marriage, Ana struggled in silence.

The school I attended, Virginia Commonwealth University, surrounds the cathedral of the Diocese of Richmond. Apparently, when the cathedral was built, some Catholics complained, wondering why the diocese would want to build a cathedral "way out in the country." Eventually, the downtown area grew to encompass the cathedral and its surroundings, now in the heart of the city. The university started on one side of the cathedral, but quickly outgrew that space and started purchasing land on the other side. Now the cathedral sits precisely in the middle of campus.

One day, as my wife and I were walking across the campus past the Cathedral of the Sacred Heart, we noticed that the very large front doors, which were usually closed and locked, were open, and so we decided to take a peek inside. There appeared to be a wedding rehearsal in progress, so we contented ourselves with a view through the glass doors. But what a view it was! Although I had been raised not to be too impressed with church buildings, the nineteenth-century French revival architecture simply took my breath away. After almost twenty-five years and lots of world travel, Richmond's Cathedral of the Sacred Heart is still one of the most beautiful churches I have ever seen. "We should come sometime when they are having Mass," I said, "so we can see it up close."

Sitting in Mass the following Sunday, I was awed by what I was experiencing: the flow of the prayers, gestures, music, homily, and Eucharistic rite; the procession of people of all backgrounds and colors lifting their hearts and voices to their Creator. It all struck me as so beautiful. And inexplicably I felt something there that I hadn't felt in a long time — God's presence. I didn't know what God was doing in a Catholic church, but I had the overwhelming sense that he was there. I decided I wanted to learn more; a short time later, I was attending RCIA inquiry (the Rite of Christian Initiation of Adults).

My approach to faith had always been very intellectual. I grew up analyzing verses of Scripture, and during my journey into the Catholic Church, I continued to do so. But there's no denying what led me to Catholicism — it was the liturgy. The *Catechism of the Catholic Church* defines *liturgy* as "the participation of the People of God in 'the work of God'" (1069). Through the liturgy, we are offered the opportunity to celebrate the mysteries of our faith, participating in "Christ's own prayer addressed to the Father in the Holy Spirit" (CCC 1073). All families have traditional ways of celebrating special times, and the Church family is no exception. Liturgy is the way our Church family worships and the way we mark important events.

One important aspect of the liturgical life of the Church is the liturgical cycle, the seasons of our faith through which we re-experience the events of salvation history over the course of the year. In Advent, we experience the promise of the Light to come. The celebration of the Incarnation in the Christmas season is a time of joy, light, and hope that calls to mind the hopes and dreams we have for our lives and for our children. These hopes are a source of strength through both the minor frustrations of everyday life and the periods of greater struggle; even in times of darkness, the promise of light brings us moments of joy.

Ordinary Time spans most of the liturgical year. It is a joyful time (we sing the "Gloria" and "Alleluia" at Mass), but without the high intensity of celebration we share at Christmas and Easter. We honor the Blessed Virgin Mary and other saints throughout the liturgical year, helping us to remember that our worship on earth is united with the liturgy of heaven (see CCC 1195). Ordinary Time reflects the everyday moments where most of our lives are lived: getting up, going to work, coming home, having dinner, spending time together as families doing ordinary things. These moments don't necessarily stand out in our memories, but they are times to find small joys, little things for which we can give thanks.

We all come to crossroads in our lives; some are marked by conflicts, goodbyes, and even tragedies. At these times, we reexamine our lives. During Lent, we are called to reflect upon our walk with God, repent of our sins, and grow in our faith through the Lenten disciplines of prayer, fasting, and almsgiving. Lent is a "darker" time that foreshadows the suffering and death of Christ. But there is light at the end of Lent.

On the other side of tragedy and loss, we can find new beginnings. The Easter Vigil that begins the next season of the Church year is all about light. The vigil begins in total darkness; we then light the "new fire" as we remember Jesus, our Light — a light that could not be extinguished by the power of sin and death, a light that forever shines through the Church. In this liturgy, we welcome those who have been called to join the Catholic Church through the Rite of Christian Initiation of Adults. It is a sign of the new life our Church has through Christ. And just as in life, those new beginnings flow again into the daily rhythm of Ordinary Time, leading into more hopes, joys, sorrows, and new beginnings. In the Catholic Church, time is not linear. It is cyclic.

At the heart of our liturgical life as a Church, we find the seven sacraments — those encounters with God in which he shares his very life with us. The sacrament most central to our worship is the one we celebrate in every Mass — the Eucharist, "the source and summit of the Christian life" (*Lumen Gentium*, 11). In the Eucharistic Liturgy, heaven and Earth become one. We lift our hearts to heaven, and we encounter the Real Presence of Jesus Christ — Body, Blood, Soul, and Divinity.

The meaning of the Mass is so incredibly profound that it cannot be fully conveyed to our senses. Much of what "cradle Catholics" know about the Mass they learned when they were young and less able to grasp profound, abstract ideas. Perhaps that is one reason why people so often feel something lacking in the Mass. Maybe it's not the Mass itself but our understanding of it that is the problem. Dr. Timothy O'Malley, director of education at the McGrath Institute for Church Life and academic director of the Notre Dame Center for Liturgy, says, "One of the key things is that the Mass is a very complex prayer. It's not just 'going for a jog,' it's going to a pretty sophisticated gym, where you actually have to know how to use the equipment. There's a lot of spiritual wealth to get from the Mass, but you have to know something about it and how to pray it well. The more you can focus on each part of the Mass so that you can enter more deeply into it, the better it is." Dr. O'Malley sees the Mass as an experience we can learn to connect with the most practical aspects of our daily lives. "The Mass helps me see my whole life as a sacrifice," he says. "The work that I do with students that I offer up at Mass, the work that I do as a parent, as a dad — my vocation is really [an] offering of love back to God, who gives me this love infinitely."

Years ago, I was at a wedding reception, a very formal affair put on by a fairly wealthy family. As the music began to play, a little girl of about four or five who was standing near the dance floor turned to a man standing nearby and said, "Dance with me, Daddy!" Eyes darting around self-consciously, he quietly said, "I don't know, sweetie." She reached her hands out toward him and with pleading eyes said, "Come on, Daddy! Please? I want to dance like we always do at home." Daddy relented and took her by the hands as she stepped up onto his shoes. She giggled as he began stepping back and forth in time to the music. The father forgot about feeling embarrassed after a few moments, and a charming scene unfolded. Eventually, he moved fast enough that the little girl fell off his shoes, so he swept her up in his arms and twirled her around in time to the music. She tilted her head back and laughed, savoring this moment, feeling like a princess.

In 2 Peter 1:4, we read that God wants us to "share in the divine nature." In other words, he wants to share himself with us. In the Catholic Church, we believe that one important way God does this is through the sacramental celebrations of the Church (see CCC 1129). Perhaps in a reaction to the superstitious beliefs that had developed among some Catholic Christians, some theologians in the years just after the Second Vatican Council downplayed God's active role in sacramental celebrations. They portrayed sacraments as special times in which we recognize what God has already done, rather than instances of God's active involvement. For example, baptism was presented as an opportunity to recognize that we are all already children of God; the Eucharist was a time to recall that God is always present to us.

These might sound like nice thoughts, but they do not represent the full teaching of the Church. Our sharing in the divine nature means that God takes an active role in our lives, especially through the sacraments. In every sacramental celebration, there are human actions and simultaneous divine actions, things we do and things God does. For some mysterious reason, God wants to work with us and through us to accomplish his will in our lives and in the world. Even though he could do anything he wanted without us, he delights in us and wants us to collaborate with him. When we participate in the sacraments, we join our will with God's. He hears us and responds. Like the little girl who danced with her father by standing on his shoes, we are not guiding God's actions in the sacraments. But we are active participants because God wills us to be. We are collaborators with the divine. He waits for us to join him in the sacraments.

Are we ready to experience his action in our lives? Do we have the courage to let ourselves go and join in the dance? All we have to do is put out our hands and say, "Dance with me, Daddy!" and God will lead us where we need to go. He sweeps us into his arms, holding us with the dignity afforded only to princes and princesses — sons and daughters of the King.

LISTENING TO GOD IN THE LITURGY

How has God spoken to you through sacramental celebrations you have experienced? Which baptisms, Eucharists, weddings, and so forth have been especially meaningful to you? Why?

What times in your life have mirrored the liturgical cycle of the Church? How might reflecting upon this idea help you enter more deeply into conversation with God in each liturgical season?

Find a good book for adults about the Mass. What is God trying to tell you right now about meeting him in the Liturgy? See how learning more about the parts of the Mass can enhance your understanding and experience of the liturgy.

Chapter 7

God Speaks to Us through Humor

Buddy was a little boy growing up in a medium-sized city on the East Coast just after World War II. He went to the Catholic school run by the cathedral in his diocese. A bit disorganized and forgetful, Buddy always looked just a little disheveled, with hair out of place (partly due to the cowlick squarely atop his head) and the shirttail of his school uniform tucked on one side but not on the other, which likely led to more than one reprimand from the teachers at his school, since a tucked-in shirt was part of the uniform code. Had he been growing up in the twenty-first century, Buddy might have been diagnosed with ADHD.

The rector of the cathedral that sponsored the school was a stern, older Irish priest. He was, by all accounts, quite serious

— a dour expression adorning his face on most occasions. In fact, if he ever cracked a smile, no one remembered it. His reputation for strictness was useful at times, as none of the students at the cathedral school ever wanted to engage in any monkey business if they thought Father might catch them. It was generally assumed that nothing good could come from crossing such a serious man.

Once they were old enough, the boys at the school each took a turn serving at the daily Mass at the cathedral, and Buddy's first turn was coming up. Understandably, Buddy's mother was concerned. She walked him through all of the things he would be doing (over and over, it seemed to Buddy), reminding him of the importance of paying attention during the Mass at which he would be serving, encouraging him to watch the altar server at the Masses they attended as a family. When the day came, she still had some anxiety as she sent him off to school. She took out her comb to straighten his hair once more (a lost cause, it seemed) and ran through his responsibilities with him one last time.

Fortunately for Buddy, the priest was in a good mood that day (relatively speaking, of course), perhaps because some renovations to the cathedral had recently been completed. The finishing touch was a large and beautiful imported rug placed in the middle of the sanctuary in front of the altar. (Some readers might remember, and others will have heard, that prior to the Second Vatican Council, the altar in most Catholic churches, including this one, was set farther back, against the wall at the back of the sanctuary space, which was marked off by the Communion rail. The faithful who gathered for Mass were seated on the other side of the rail. The priest said the Mass facing away from the people and toward the altar.) In this very large cathedral, there was quite a bit of space between the altar and the Communion rail, and this was where the new rug was placed, about where the altar would be today. The aesthetically minded priest felt it broke up the empty space and perfectly complemented the beauty of the altar behind it.

One of Buddy's responsibilities at Mass that day was to be in charge of the censer — to make sure the coals inside were burning, to scoop the appropriate amount of incense on top of them, and finally to lower the perforated lid on the chains that threaded through it so that it fit securely over the solid bottom bowl, allowing the smoke of the incense to escape as the priest swung the censer. Buddy did all of this with ease — or so it seemed. But when he lowered the lid of the censer, it was just slightly askew as he handed it to the priest at the appropriate time. The priest, not noticing Buddy's subtle oversight, took the censer and began to swing it. One small lit coal escaped its compartment and landed squarely in the middle of the new, expensive, imported carpet. Unaware of this small catastrophe, the priest turned toward the altar and began to pray the Mass.

Buddy, from his vantage point, was positioned perfectly to see the single wisp of smoke that rose from the place on the rug where the lit coal continued to burn. He began to try to get the priest's attention. "Father?" Buddy whispered as the priest continued to say the words of the Mass. And then a little louder as the situation grew more urgent: "Father! Father!" Eyebrows furrowed, the priest quickly turned around and tersely, almost spitting the words between his teeth, asked, "What IS it, boy?" Buddy pointed to what was now a small inferno in the middle of the precious new rug.

With a gasp, the priest ran over to the blaze. (Here, it's important to note that, in such a large cathedral, the people attending the Mass were some distance from the sanctuary and therefore would not have seen that the rug was burning. The smoke that hung in the air could very well have come from the censer itself, and so the faithful did not realize anything was amiss until they saw their pastor, who was ordinarily quite reserved, unexpectedly dash to the middle of the carpet and jump up and down, looking as if he were dancing an Irish jig.) Once the fire was out, the priest turned back toward the altar and resumed the liturgy as if nothing at all had happened.

Given his short attention span, on most days Buddy wished Mass wasn't so long. Today, as he looked over at the scorched hole in the rug, Buddy hoped it would be a long while before he had to walk back to the sacristy with Father, as he had *no idea* what the punishment might be for starting a fire in the middle of Mass. That was something even the worst-behaved kids at school had never done. But the end of Mass came. As Buddy walked back to the sacristy, he felt as if he were walking the plank on a pirate ship. A single bead of sweat rolled down the side of his face as he thought to himself, "They'll never let me serve at Mass again. They probably won't even let me be Catholic anymore." Just after Buddy and the priest stepped into the sacristy, the priest turned around and looked Buddy square in the eye. Every muscle in Buddy's body tensed as he held his breath and prepared himself for what was to come.

And then something unexpected happened. The priest's face broke into a smile. In his Irish lilt he said, "Oh, we gave 'em a good show today, didn't we, Buddy?" and dissolved into laughter. After Buddy caught his breath again, he laughed as well.

Humor is a great gift from God. It brings loved ones closer together, giving them stories to tell and memories to cherish. It lightens our load in difficult times, softening the physical and emotional blows life can sometimes deal us. Humor can even end arguments and help to mend friendships. It's so important that we find the time and the opportunity to share a laugh together. Laughter is part of what it means to be human.

Jesus was both fully God and fully human, and he certainly

had a sense of humor. While the Gospel writers don't focus a great deal on Jesus' sense of humor, we see glimpses of it in the Gospels. Imagine Jesus in Matthew 22:15–22 as he is asked whether it is lawful to pay taxes to Caesar. I like to think he smiled as he requested that someone bring him a coin and asked, "Whose image is this?" Clearly, he knew, and so did everyone in the crowd. Jesus was making a joke. Caesar's picture is on it, so it must be his. Give him what is his, and give to God what belongs to him! On another occasion (see Mt 11:25), Jesus seems to find it humorous that the educated people listening to him preach, the scribes and Pharisees, seem confused by his message, and yet the simplest people in the crowd grasp his meaning. He praises God for revealing his truth to the simple ones and hiding it from the wise. Jesus sees the irony in the moment and has a little laugh. Elsewhere in the Gospels, when James and John want Jesus to call down fire and brimstone on a town after the people do not accept his message (Lk 9:54), he nicknames them "Sons of Thunder" (Mk 3:17). If we look for it, we can see the humor of Jesus throughout the Gospels. So why do people assume that to be holy is to be somber?

Pope Francis has pointed out the importance of Christians being joyful and having a healthy sense of humor, not just for themselves, but also for the witness they show to the world. In his apostolic exhortation *Evangelii Gaudium* (The Joy of the Gospel), Pope Francis cautions us not to be "sourpusses" (85). The Spanish term he uses is *cara de vinagre*, or "vinegar face," which paints a vivid picture. Nobody is going to look at a "vinegar face" and think, "I need what they've got." To be witnesses of Christ, we must be joyful, and to be joyful, we need a sense of humor.

Pope Francis begins every day with the Prayer of Saint Thomas More for Good Humor. I think it's an excellent prayer for all of us to pray:

Grant me, O Lord, good digestion, and also
  something to digest.
Grant me a healthy body, and the necessary
  good humor to maintain it.
Grant me a simple soul that knows to treasure
  all that is good
and that doesn't frighten easily at the sight of
  evil,
but rather finds the means to put things back
  in their place.
Give me a soul that knows not boredom,
  grumblings, sighs and laments,
nor excess of stress, because of that obstructing
  thing called "I."
Grant me, O Lord, a sense of good humor.
Allow me the grace to be able to take a joke, to
  discover in life a bit of joy,
and to be able to share it with others.

I'm grateful that, despite his reputation, that stern old Irish priest
in the cathedral so many years ago was given the grace to find
humor in a difficult situation. It taught Buddy a lesson he would
never forget: that everyone, despite their imperfections, is welcome in Christ's Church. Buddy continued to serve at the altar,
and he even grew up to be a priest — Monsignor Charles Kelly,
who a generation later would himself be the rector of that very
same cathedral, the Cathedral of the Sacred Heart in Richmond,
Virginia. And it was Monsignor Kelly who led me into the Catholic Church. In his warmth and humor, I could hear God telling
me that I was welcome, even with my doubts and questions.

Monsignor Kelly died just four years after my reception into
the Church. At his funeral Mass, the cathedral was filled with
people from all over the diocese and from neighboring states —

both clergy and laity — who wanted to honor this man who had a reputation for not taking himself too seriously, for welcoming everyone, and for being a living witness of the joy of the Lord.

LISTENING FOR GOD IN HUMOR

Pray the Prayer of Saint Thomas More for Good Humor that appears toward the end of this chapter. Which of the petitions in this prayer are particularly challenging for you?

Read the Gospel passages that are cited in this chapter. Can you picture Jesus sharing a laugh with his listeners?

Chapter 8
God Speaks to Us through Our Gifts and Talents

Shortly after I entered the Catholic Church, our director of religious education announced at Mass one Sunday that they still needed catechists for second grade for the upcoming year. At the time, Ana was an early childhood teacher, and I was a graduate student studying child psychology. We looked at each other, thinking that perhaps we should volunteer, but decided to wait and see if they found anyone else. Week after week, we kept hearing the same announcement: "We still need catechists for second grade." They weren't going to find anyone else. God was calling us to volunteer.

We soon found out why this particular volunteer position was so hard to fill: The second grade class, it turned out, had a reputation. They had been together since prekindergarten and were the noisiest, most active group in the parish's religious education program. Each year, when they moved up a grade, it seemed that the catechist for that grade decided he or she needed to take a year off. This year was no exception.

Our first day with this group was a whirlwind. This was a cast of characters — very talkative and always moving. The most active of all was a little boy named Robert, tall and thin with reddish-blond hair and freckles. He was probably thin because he was in constant motion. And when I say constant motion, I mean like what happens when you hit a racquetball as hard as you can against one wall of a racquetball court. Know how the ball bounces all around — ceiling to wall to floor to ceiling? That was Robert. A little human racquetball. He was constantly zipping around the room, and if we turned our backs to him, we might turn back around to find him on top of one of the tables. If we asked him what he was doing there, he wouldn't remember. When we could get him seated, he was always the first to jump into whatever supplies were out on the tables, even before directions were given, and then he would get frustrated when his project didn't turn out right. In class discussions, Robert would often talk right over someone else. It seemed he had never heard of raising your hand or taking turns when speaking. That said, Robert seemed to *want* to do a good job. He was always redirectable, would always apologize, and would always settle down when asked. Just not for long.

We knew that a traditional catechetical session was not going to hold this group's attention. Ana pulled out all her best teacher tricks — multisensory adaptations, hands-on activities, and music. I implemented my best behavioral interventions, including reinforcing the positive that we saw, modeling participation, and identifying and capitalizing on strengths. We relied a lot on looking for good things we saw kids doing and pointing them out, and we began, over time, to call out the gifts that we saw. One child named Elizabeth loved to sing; she was always the first to come to our music circle, and she sang out to each song. Jackson loved animals and always remembered to pray for people who had no food to eat. We also had the junior scholars, Ariana and Jacob, whose hands shot up every time we asked a question. Although their answers were usually correct, we tried to encourage at least some attempts from others in the group.

After several months of focusing on the positive, our group grew into a cohesive family of engaged learners. It's a principle of behavioral psychology that behaviors that we positively reinforce will increase over time, but I choose to think that something else was also at work here. I believe that when we discover the gifts and talents God has given others and point them out, we are looking at them the way God does, with eyes that see their goodness and potential. And we are encouraging those whose gifts we name to look at themselves the same way.

I saw this play out one year in vacation Bible school when I was working with a mixed-age crew of elementary students. From the very first day, a fourth grader named Sarah dominated the group. She monopolized group discussions, and when she was responsible for project supplies, she took the best for herself before passing them to the other kids. During our snack break in the middle of the last day of VBS week, I named a gift I saw in each of the kids that week. One girl who was younger than the rest and very shy early in the week had come out of her shell and participated well in the week. I told her she had the gift of courage. Caleb, who happened to be the oldest group member, showed empathy to the other children and was particularly helpful throughout the week. I named compassion as one of his gifts. Logan had severe allergies and was often sniffling during and after our outdoor activities, but he powered through and enjoyed himself anyway. I told him I noticed the determination God had given him. For Sarah, I named the gift of leadership, with the addendum that to use the gift of leadership well, we had to be mindful of others. "A good leader thinks about the needs and notices the feelings of everyone in the group," I said.

That afternoon, I was leading the group in a discussion of one of the lessons. Feeling pressed for time after a couple of the children had answered, I tried to move on, but Sarah quickly interjected, "Wait a minute, Logan didn't get to answer, and I think he wanted to." I smiled. Sarah was already refining her gifts as a leader. The gifts and talents God gives us are often diamonds in the rough — we have lessons to learn before we can use them well. But we can't learn the lessons until we name the gifts.

At the end of the year in that rambunctious second-grade class, Ana and I decided to highlight the gifts we had seen in the children over the course of the year with a special awards ceremony. We went to our local Catholic bookstore, bought as many different saint medals as we could find, and then started to match each saint with a child who shared some of the talents and gifts demonstrated in the life of that saint. For example, we matched Elizabeth, who loved to sing, with Saint Cecilia. Jackson (the child who loved animals and prayed for the poor) was a natural for the Saint Francis award. Our junior scholars, Ariana and Jacob, were perfect for the Saint Teresa of Ávila and Saint Thomas Aquinas awards. And then we came to Robert. What saint award could we give to Robert? Looking at the remaining medals, we suddenly recognized a saint who was full of energy and enthusiasm but also impulsive, one who spoke out of turn sometimes and put his foot in his mouth. He was the first to jump out of the boat when Jesus walked on water, but he got distracted by the wind and waves and began to sink. If there was a patron saint of ADHD, it had to be — you guessed it — Saint Peter!

After we matched each saint medal with the child who would receive it, we tied them on pieces of cord, prepared certificates for each child, and planned what we would say. We wrote a short speech for each award, first introducing the saint and his or her qualities, then talking about the child and the talents and gifts he or she shared with the saint, then naming the child. We asked the parents to come to the classroom thirty minutes early to witness their children receiving special awards.

We bestowed the awards one by one, reading the speech, inviting each child to come up and receive his or her medal and certificate, and usually posing for a photo or two. Finally, we got to Robert. Here's what we said:

> Saint Peter was full of energy. He was bold and ready — always the first to jump into whatever Jesus had planned. Jesus knew it would take someone with Saint Peter's courage and energy to lead the Church after he went back to heaven to be with the Father, so he made Saint Peter our first pope. We have someone in our class who is full of energy. He's always ready to jump into whatever we have planned. We know that God must have big plans for him, too. The Saint Peter award goes to ... Robert!

We hadn't fully anticipated Robert's reaction to receiving this award. You know those moments in movies and TV shows when it seems that a beam of light comes down out of nowhere and one of the characters just begins to glow? That was what Robert looked like in that moment. He just lit up. He looked to be ten feet off the ground as he walked with a huge smile to the front of the room to receive his award. Only then did I realize that Robert probably hadn't ever received an award before.

A couple of years later, after I had finished graduate school and we had moved across the country, we received a Christmas card from Robert's family. The card read, "Robert still thinks of you often, and he wears his Saint Peter medal every day." Inside the card was a picture of Robert, now in fourth grade, wearing a soccer uniform and the Saint Peter medal around his neck. Three or four years later, when Robert was in middle school, we received another Christmas card from his family. "Robert's Saint Peter medal oxidized and fell apart a while back," it read, "but we got him a sterling silver one, and he still wears it every day." Robert's identification with a saint who shared his gifts was so strong that he wore that Saint Peter medal wherever he went. To him, it was an affirmation that what he brings to the world, and to the Church, is important and needed.

We often ask children and teens what they want to be or do when they grow up. While our passions and dreams might be important signs of what God has called us to, they are not the only signs. Each of us is unique and unrepeatable. God gives every one of us a unique combination of gifts to help us fulfill our God-given mission. Perhaps we should start asking children, "What do you think God made you to do?" or "What is God's dream for your life?" I think that sometimes we are afraid to ask young people these kinds of questions. Will it put too much pressure on them? Many parents say that the most important thing for them is that their children are happy. But we don't always know what will make us happy. Sometimes we chase dreams and then find that we are left feeling hollow when we reach our goals. Somehow, achieving what we set out to do didn't quite bring us the fulfillment we thought it would. The happiest, the most fulfilled we can be is when we are doing what we were created to do. In fact, when we discover something we do really well, something that gives us real joy, we often say, "I was made for this."

The talents we recognize in ourselves, or that other people recognize in us, is often one way God speaks to us about the vocation, or calling, he has given us. To follow this calling, to fully embrace it, is to begin a journey down the road to being fully alive.

For we can only find authentic happiness and freedom when we become the people we were meant to be — perfectly ourselves.

LISTENING FOR GOD IN THE GIFTS AND TALENTS HE HAS GIVEN US

What are some of the things you really enjoy doing? What are you best at?

What gifts have other people recognized in you?

How can you use the talents God has given you in your family, your parish, your workplace, and your community?

Chapter 9

God Speaks to Us through the Saints

We were scheduled to go on one of our mission trips to the rain forest. This was an important one: We were beginning an education project with the Emberá tribe — an idea that came from them after several conversations about the best way for us to partner with their village. We also planned to hold some faith formation activities for the children. We knew the parents would attend as well, so this would be a great opportunity to evangelize the whole community. The supplies were all packed, the plane tickets bought. There was just one problem — we couldn't get in contact with them. If they didn't know we were coming, there was simply no good way to get there. The community is so isolated that reaching it requires being piloted by canoe quite some distance up the river, and we had never gone to the village without an Emberá guide to lead us.

We began the difficult process of discerning whether to cancel the trip. We started a novena to Saint Thérèse of Lisieux, one of my favorite saints, who also happens to be the patron saint of missionaries. Although she spent almost all her life in one small town in northwestern France, she dreamed of traveling the world telling others about Jesus. As a child, she drew a map of North America because she dreamed of visiting this faraway place to spread the Gospel.

As she grew to understand her vocation, Thérèse realized that she was called not to evangelize in faraway lands but to serve God in small, everyday ways as a cloistered religious sister in the Carmelite convent near her family home. Reflecting on Saint Paul's exhortation "whatever you do, do everything for the glory of God" (1 Cor 10:31), she made it her mission to work for Jesus in the smallest of actions, practicing a spirituality she called her "Little Way" to heaven. She said, "Jesus does not pay as much attention to the greatness of our acts, or even how difficult they are, as to the love that motivates them" (letter to her sister Céline, October 20, 1888). In Thérèse, many Catholic faithful have found a simple, accessible kind of holiness — a way to follow God's will whoever and wherever you are.

As her life drew to an end, Thérèse seemed to have an increasing realization that she would do in death what she could not do in life. On her deathbed near the end of a long period of suffering with tuberculosis, she said, "I feel that my mission is about to begin — to make others love God as I love Him" (*Last Conversations*, July 17, 1897). Thérèse promised to spend her heaven "doing good on earth." Her autobiography, *The Story of a Soul* (written at her sister and mother superior's insistence) was published posthumously and became an instant classic of Catholic spirituality. Thérèse was proclaimed "Doctor of the Church" by Pope John Paul II in 1997, one hundred years after her death.

Not only have her writings changed countless lives, but many people have attributed answered prayers to her intercession.

It was nearing the end of our novena to Saint Thérèse, and we still had not received any clear sign that our trip to the rain forest was going to work out. With a heavy heart, I headed in to work at the diocesan offices, where I was greeted by Charlene, a friend and coworker who knew of our plans to leave on a mission trip but had not heard about the complications we were facing. "I have something for you," she said, and handed me a very old looking *theca* (relic holder). "Saint Thérèse wants to go with you to Panama." Breathless, I realized she had just given me a first-class relic of Saint Thérèse. Charlene had gotten the relic, a lock of Thérèse's hair, from a convent that had recently closed. In the preceding days, she had had the overwhelming feeling that she should give it to my wife and me.

Needless to say, we took this as a clear sign that we were meant to take the trip after all. I'll admit to feeling a little nervous when we were at the gate about to board our plane and still hadn't heard from our Emberá friends. But just as the gate agent began the boarding process, my cell phone rang. Our friends told us that the one satellite phone in the village, the only phone that could call the outside world, had just been fixed after being down for several days. We quickly made arrangements to meet near the river, and the next day, we were headed into the rainforest to be with our friends once again. It was one of our most memorable and meaningful trips. Saint Thérèse was certainly with us the whole way.

In a certain sense, "the Church" and the "communion of saints" are one and the same (see CCC 946). For the Church is the People of God, both the living and those who have died in Christ. The "oneness" of the Church is so powerful that even time and death do not separate its members. We are forever united to those who have gone before us and those who will come after us in the Faith. The *Catechism*, with guidance from the Second Vatican Council's Dogmatic Constitution on the Church, *Lumen Gentium*, describes how living and deceased members of the Church are separated yet united:

> At the present time some of his disciples are pilgrims on earth. Others have died and are being purified, while still others are in glory, contemplating "in full light, God himself triune and one, exactly as he is":
>
>> All of us, however, in varying degrees and in different ways share in the same charity towards God and our neighbours, and we all sing the one hymn of glory to our God. All, indeed, who are of Christ and who have his Spirit form one Church and in Christ cleave together. (954)

Sometimes my non-Catholic friends and family members will ask me, "Why do you Catholics pray to the saints? Can't you just talk directly to God?" The answer to the second question is of course yes, but there is something comforting and powerful about being joined in prayer by someone we know is close to God. Curiously, if I ask these friends and family members to pray for me, they never refuse and say I can go directly to God. So why can't we also ask our brothers and sisters in heaven to pray for us? According to the *Catechism*, our brothers and sisters who have died and are now united more closely with Christ offer prayers for us to the Father (956). While we can certainly approach God directly, it makes sense to ask the saints to intercede for us because they are able to see things from a perspective that is freer from selfish interests and material concerns. "The fervent prayer of a righteous person is very powerful" (Jas 5:16).

Saint Polycarp was bishop of Smyrna (now part of Turkey) in the late first and early second century. He is believed to have been a disciple of John the Evangelist. He was a powerful defender of the Faith in the face of early heresies, and he wrote a letter to the Philippian church that survives to this day. This was a time of great persecution of the Church, and Christians were often tortured and killed in front of large crowds for entertainment. Polycarp was arrested by Roman officials around the year 155. Although as a bishop, Polycarp was quite a prize, the Roman proconsul felt sorry for him due to his advanced age. He therefore offered Polycarp a way out, saying that he would be freed if he would renounce Christ and pledge his loyalty to Caesar. Polycarp replied, "Eighty and six years have I served him, and he hath done me no wrong; how then can I blaspheme my king who saved me?" (*Martyrium Polycarpi*, 9). With these words, Polycarp signed his death sentence … and secured his place in heaven. The most complete account of Polycarp's martyrdom says that the officials first tried to burn him at the stake. This was unsuccessful — for some reason, his body would not burn, though onlookers reported an unusual smell like baking bread. Having failed to kill him by fire, the soldiers plunged a knife in his chest and stabbed him to death. With that, Polycarp left this world and entered eternal life in heaven.

In a time when there seems to be a shortage of real heroes, when our young people find their role models in video gamers on YouTube and fashionistas on Instagram, we are challenged and inspired by stories of great saints like Thérèse and Polycarp. In their lives, God speaks to us about what the Gospel looks like when it is lived by real human beings, with all their imperfections. In the saints, we find inspiration to live everyday lives of holiness and to stay close enough to Jesus to rise to the occasion if we're called to sacrifice everything. In them, we also find friends who hear us and pray for us.

In the eleventh chapter of the Letter to the Hebrews, the writer describes several people of faith, including Abel, Noah, Abraham and Sarah, Isaac and Jacob, Joseph, Moses, and Rahab. Then, at the beginning of chapter 12, we find these words: "Therefore, since we are surrounded by so great a cloud of witnesses, let us rid ourselves of every burden and sin that clings to us and persevere in running the race that lies before us" (Heb 12:1). Did you catch that? Scripture is describing a scene in which we are running a race, and those who have gone before us are in the stands, cheering us on. If we are "surrounded by ... a cloud of witnesses," then our friends in heaven are not only heroes and examples to us, they are companions on our journey. Let us remember them, talk to them, and listen to what their lives tell us about how to be the best versions of ourselves.

LISTENING FOR GOD IN THE SAINTS

Who is your favorite saint? How has God spoken to you through this saint?

Choose a moment of your everyday routine that you find especially tedious or trying. How does completing this task as if working for God himself change your experience?

In what ways are you called to stand up for what you believe in today's world? How might stories of saints like Polycarp provide inspiration and courage?

Chapter 10

God Speaks to Us through the Arts

The Last Supper by Leonardo da Vinci is one of the world's most famous paintings, but it isn't easy to see. It's not in a museum; it was painted on the wall of an old monastery dining room at Santa Maria delle Grazie Church in Milan. Only twenty to twenty-five people can see the painting at a time, and one can stay for a maximum of fifteen minutes. It sounds like a short time, but there are only two paintings in the old dining hall — *The Last Supper* and a painting of the crucifixion by Giovanni Donato da Montorfano. The latter is a beautiful painting in its own right, but it is surely underappreciated because it stands in the shadow of one of the greatest masterpieces of all time.

To see *The Last Supper*, you must have advance tickets.

Because of the space limitations, the tickets generally sell out weeks, if not months, in advance. When you arrive for your date with Leonardo's painting, you first spend some time in a waiting area. When it's almost time for you to see the painting, you move into a small, climate-controlled room with a bulletproof glass door. The buildup, of course, adds to your awareness that you are about to see something very, very important. Just after the group ahead of you exits, the door on the other side of the small holding cell slides open, and you walk into the hall.

The painting is quite large, taking up almost a whole wall. As you gaze upon Jesus and the disciples, you will notice something that is visible, but not nearly so obvious, in the countless images and prints you have seen of the painting: There is a door, now sealed, cut into the wall under the table just below the figure of Christ. When Leonardo painted his depiction of the Last Supper, the monks in the monastery still ate all their meals in the dining hall. On the other side of the wall he painted was the kitchen. Apparently, the cooks got tired of walking outside to transport food from the kitchen to the dining room, so they cut a doorway into the wall — right through one of the world's most famous works of art. To be fair, way back then, the monks probably didn't realize how greatly Leonardo's work would be treasured. In any case, the door has been there for nearly four hundred years, and it's in every image you have seen, so it doesn't really detract from the experience.

The first time I saw *The Last Supper*, it was amazing; there's something truly special about seeing something you have only seen photos of all your life. But my second visit there, just a year later, was even better. This time, the guide who took us inside to view the painting gave us two pieces of advice that turned out to be very important. "Most people who come to view the painting," she said, "walk right up to the railing so they can see it up close. But try something different. Step back about three-fourths of the length of the room, and see what happens." I followed her advice, and to my amazement, the painting suddenly became three-dimensional. Leonardo was such a master of perspective that he could make this scene of Jesus' last meal with his disciples appear to come to life before your very eyes. The guide gave us one more piece of advice: "Pay attention to the expressions on the faces of the disciples. The moment Leonardo is capturing is the one just after Jesus has said that one of his disciples would betray him. They are all reacting in different ways to this revelation by their teacher. I like to imagine myself as one of the disciples. See which one you connect most with."

Scanning the painting from left to right, my eyes settled on Saint Philip, who stands with his hands pointing in toward his chest. "Is it me, Lord?" he seems to ask, "Am I the one who will betray you?" In this moment in which some of the disciples are shocked, some are outraged, and some are saddened, Philip doubts himself, acutely aware of his weaknesses and limitations. How I identify with Philip in this painting! Even as I write these chapters on listening to God, I hear an inner voice that tells me I'm entirely unqualified to write such a book. But in that moment in Milan, as I gazed upon Philip and his reaction to our Lord, it was comforting to feel that even in my self-doubt, I was in good company.

The arts have an extraordinary power to evoke emotion and to provoke reflection. Beauty is one of the three "transcendentals," properties of being that can lift human consciousness toward something beyond ourselves. The Catholic Church has been a patron and promoter of the arts throughout the ages, commissioning beautiful architecture, stained glass windows, icons, statues, paintings, frescoes, and beautiful music that teach us about our faith and direct our minds and senses toward the sacred — toward heaven. Leonardo Defilippis, who is director of the 2004 film *Thérèse* and president of Saint Luke Productions, the longest-running Catholic theater group in the United States, points out that art "is a huge influence in the culture and on the culture." What art is about, says Defilippis, is expressing themes of "good and evil, truth and falsehood, life and death, clarity and confusion, order and chaos."

Defilippis calls film an art form that is "very powerful ... seductive. It pulls you in. You are a spectator ... immersed in a visual reality." An advantage of film as an art form, he says, is its power to reach many people at once. Live drama, on the other hand, Defilippis notes, is unique "because it's ancient. It's connected to human experience in a different way. It's the only art form that combines all into one — visual, auditory, and movement. It has the greatest impact because it uses all the senses. Historically," he says, "theatre has had a great impact," even to the point of "causing revolutions." Defilippis also contends that drama imitates the ministry of Jesus in a particular way "because he did everything live."

Saint Luke Productions started with a dramatization of the Gospel of Luke and has since also presented a dramatic adaptation of the Gospel of John. The company currently tours with five plays based on the lives of saints. Defilippis describes the effect on the audience of a live performance of Scripture as "mysterious." While people react in various ways, he says, for some it reaffirms the Faith. The effect of the saint dramas can be different. "People don't know the saints," Defilippis says, or at least "they don't know them as people." When people see the life of a saint portrayed in a dramatic fashion, "they feel like they are meeting that person. It's very intimate, but also intimidating." Some people, Defilippis says, break down crying, overwhelmed with emotion as they witness the story of a hero of faith in such a powerful medium. It can also have a significant effect on the actor, he explains, citing the example of Jim Coleman, star of one of his current productions on the life of Father Augustus Tolton.

Coleman, Defilippis notes, has been successful as a television star, but has said that his role as Father Tolton has been the most important work in his thirty-year career.

No discussion of the way God speaks to us through the arts would be complete without mention of the significant role music has played, and continues to play, in our religious imagination and experience. Some of the most renowned pieces of music ever composed were written for religious purposes. The world's greatest composers have often produced music to worship the Creator.

John Burland, a Catholic composer and musician from Australia, describes his work as a personal act of worship and connection with God: "For me music has been a powerful way to express my faith and belief in God. It wipes away the busyness of each day and allows me to clearly hear God's voice and feel God's presence in my life. By singing a particular song or taking the words from my own personal prayer and adding a simple melody, I'm immediately reassured and calmed by God's love, comfort, and strength."

Burland points to one of his songs in particular, "Lord Bless Me on This Day," as his "own personal prayer set to music":

> Lord bless me on this day
> Guide me in your way
> Calm my mind to be
> Let my eyes now see
> Surround me
> Surround me
> Surround me with Your love
>
> When I wander far from you
> Be with me O Lord
> When I don't know what to do
> Be with me O Lord

When I need to trust in You
Be with me O Lord
When I doubt my faith in You
Be with me O Lord

When I'm weary from the day
Be with me O Lord
When I haven't lived Your way
Be with me O Lord*

Many of Burland's songs are based in Scripture, and he says he experiences God speaking to him when he performs them: "I clearly hear God's voice and I'm reminded what I have been asked by God to do … and what God has called me to be."

Much of Burland's work is with children, and he describes the unique impact music can have on young souls: "Whether it is a group of 20 or 1,000 children, music unites and becomes a powerful vehicle for prayer. Standing up at the front and looking out at an audience, you can see and feel that the children aren't just singing your song — they are praying it, deeply absorbing each word, listening to each other. United as one voice their song becomes a communal prayer to God." Burland notes that the music's power to unite a group of children is evident as well in its unique ability to be inclusive, especially of children with diverse needs, including those with disabilities:

> Often when I travel to a school community, I'll be told by one of the teachers that there are some children who will just come in for a little while as they have significant diverse learning needs. After a brief conversation I assure the teacher that I would like these students to be

---

* John Burland, "Lord Bless Me on This Day," lyrics used with permission.

present and involved. In nearly every single case these children are totally and actively involved for the whole concert ... to the amazement of their teacher. For me, as I look out and see them singing, moving, interacting with joy and enthusiasm, it is a sacred and humbling experience as it is clear that God is touching them by these songs.

The arts can inspire, energize, unite, and mobilize. Perhaps nothing else in our everyday lives has the power that the arts have to reach a large and diverse audience, communicate a message, and evoke emotion. Present in every culture (in fact, sociologists say that it is one of the characteristics that define culture), art is a reflection of the deepest longings and strivings of the human spirit. God speaks to us through the arts — the beauty we find in a visual masterpiece points us to the divine. The experience of making music and praising God together helps us feel his presence. The emotion we experience when we watch a play or film dramatizing Scripture or the life of a saint inspires us. The highest form of art, Defilippis argues, is one that is directed toward oneness with God: "The greatest art will help us prepare for eternal life."

LISTENING FOR GOD IN THE ARTS

What visual artwork, song, film, or play has spoken to you about faith? What did you hear God saying to you through this work of art?

What has been your personal experience in the arts? Do you have any particular talents in drawing, painting, drama, music, or other art forms? How can you experience God's presence in this medium and help others do the same?

Chapter 11

God Speaks to Us in Sacred Tradition and Sacred Scripture

One of my earliest memories is of my grandma reading her Bible each night before she went to bed. I don't remember her ever saying anything about what she was doing, but every night I can recall staying at my grandparents' house as a child, she sat at the kitchen table, spending time in God's Word. It really made an impression on me: If this book was important enough for my grandma to take time out every night to read it, there must be something truly special about it.

Throughout my undergraduate years and into my first year of graduate school, I was searching. I had grown up in the Church of Christ, an evangelical Protestant denomination. I am grateful for the many gifts I received there, including a love of Scripture and an understanding of other Christians as my brothers and sisters. However, in my teenage years, like many adolescents, I began to question some of the tenets of my faith. The Church of Christ was established during the "Restoration Movement" of the early 1800s. Its founders had become disillusioned by all the different branches of Protestant Christianity and decided to go back to basics. Adopting the model "Speak where the Bible speaks, and be silent where the Bible is silent," they set out to form congregations that could include all followers of Jesus, without all the "silly traditions" that had divided Christians over the years. The problem was, absent any external authority, even the early leaders of this movement couldn't agree on exactly what the Bible said (and meant) or on what was essential and what wasn't. And so, almost as soon as this movement toward Christian unity began, it fractured into smaller sects that couldn't worship together. My church was one of the fruits of that initial division.

When I started attending RCIA inquiry at a Catholic church, I told my wife that I would be out of there the first time they said something that was "against the Bible." I wasn't sure what it would be, but I suspected it would be something about Mary or the pope. As it turned out, not only did I discover that the Catholic Church didn't teach "against the Bible," but I came to understand that it was the Church through which the Bible came. I understood Scripture much better when I understood the context in which it had been written. Passages that had never made sense to me before finally had meaning in light of the Tradition of the Church.

God has chosen to reveal himself to humanity gradually, first through covenants with his people (e.g., his promises to Noah, Abraham, and Moses), and most completely in the Person of Jesus Christ. Jesus is the last and definitive Word of God to humanity; there is no better way for God to show us who he is than in the Person of Jesus. Since the time of Christ, God's Revelation has been passed on in two ways — orally (through Sacred Tradition) and in written form (Sacred Scripture).

While we can hear the voice of God in our lives in many different ways (including those discussed in the previous chapters of this book), Sacred Scripture and Sacred Tradition offer us a sure standard for discerning the will of God. They can serve as a compass to keep us on track: If we feel God is leading us in a certain direction, but discover that this direction is contradictory to God's Revelation in Sacred Scripture and Sacred Tradition, then we know it's time to reevaluate.

Catholics read Scripture a little differently than some Christians do. However, we do believe that Sacred Scripture is inspired by God and that the Bible is different from any other book because it contains the Word of God. The Word came through human authors, and the writings of Scripture bear the characteristics of their human authors. Still, the *Catechism of the Catholic Church* teaches that "the books of Scripture firmly, faithfully, and without error teach that truth which God, for the sake of our salvation, wished to see confided to the Sacred Scriptures" (107).

To preserve the purity of the Gospel message, God gave the Church the gift of apostolic succession. Jesus chose twelve apostles to spread his message. When Judas, out of his own free will, chose to betray Jesus and later took his own life, the other eleven Apostles, under the inspiration of the Holy Spirit, selected another disciple to replace him (see Acts 1:15–26). This tradition of choosing successors to the apostles has continued to this day, and our contemporary bishops (including the pope) represent an unbroken line of apostolic succession throughout the centuries. This point is important for a number of reasons.

First of all, the New Testament as we know it did not exist for the first few hundred years of the life of the Church. There were literally hundreds of manuscripts about Christ and the Church, creating some confusion about which writings were truly the Word of God. In the year 367, Saint Athanasius proposed a definitive list of the books of the New Testament. His list was adopted by Pope Saint Damasus I in 382 and confirmed by a council of Catholic bishops in 419. For the next thousand years, until the invention of the printing press, books of Scripture were still unavailable to most Christians. All this is to say that a Church built on Scripture alone would have been impossible. Moreover, Scripture can be interpreted in different ways by sincere people, resulting in literally tens of thousands of Christian sects.

Christian unity is another reason that apostolic succession is important. On the night before Jesus died, his fervent prayer was that all of his followers would be one (see Jn 17:20–21). I'm struck by several implications of this prayer of Jesus. First, Jesus knew he was about to be handed over to die, and yet his concern was about the unity of his followers. This means that our unity, our "oneness" with Christ and with one another, is important. Second, Jesus would not have prayed to the Father for something that was impossible. If there was no way for Christians to be unified, Jesus wouldn't have prayed for it. Finally, if unity was so important to Jesus, he wouldn't have left his followers without a *means* to stay unified.

This points to the necessity of apostolic succession and Sacred Tradition. The Church relied on Sacred Tradition to guide her through the first centuries of her existence. She relied on the Magisterium (the teaching authority passed down from the apostles to the pope and his fellow bishops) to know which books of Scripture were divinely inspired. We continue to rely on Sacred Tradition and the teaching authority of the Magisterium to interpret Scripture in the modern world. Sacred Tradition is the context in which Scripture arose and the context in which it must be interpreted. It is the means through which Christian unity is possible.

How can we hear the message God wishes to speak to us through Scripture? Saint Paul called the Church the "pillar and foundation of truth" (1 Tm 3:15). Let's look at how the Church teaches us to interpret Scripture:

- **Take into account the time period, culture, and kind of writing.** While the meaning of Sacred Scripture is timeless, each book of the Bible was written in a particular time, culture, and style (see CCC 110). For example, some parts of the Bible are letters from one person to another or to groups of people, others are written accounts of events that occurred in the lives of God's people, and still other portions of Scripture are poems and songs. The Holy Spirit inspired all the biblical authors, who lived in particular times and cultural contexts, to write what God willed for us to learn through the Scriptures.

- **Read parts of Scripture in the context of the whole message.** The Bible contains parts that vary in style and tone, but it is unified because the parts all point toward God's Divine Plan, with Jesus Christ as the center and heart (CCC 112).

- **"Read Scripture within 'the living Tradition of the whole Church'"** (CCC 113). It's important to remember that as Catholics, we base our faith not on a book but on the living Word of God, which is present in both Scripture and Sacred Tradition (see 2 Thes 2:15). We understand God's Word not only through Scripture but also through the many people who have wisely taught Scripture through the generations.

- **Pay special attention to the truths of faith expressed in Scripture.** Great truths are always consistent with one another. For example, both the Old and New Testaments present love for God and love for one's neighbor as guiding principles of God's law.

- **Know the senses of Scripture.** To truly understand Scripture, we should pay attention to both its literal and spiritual senses (CCC 115). There are three categories of the spiritual sense (117):

  1. *The allegorical sense*: An allegory uses characters or events to symbolize an idea or principle. The *Catechism* speaks of the crossing of the Red Sea as an allegory of baptism. The Israelites crossed the Red Sea to freedom from captivity in Egypt. We enter into the waters of baptism and are freed from the captivity of sin.

  2. *The moral sense*: The moral sense of Scripture is the way in which it teaches us lessons about right and wrong.

  3. *The anagogical sense*: This gives us signs of eternal things. For example, the *Catechism* points out that the Church on earth is a sign of God's eternal kingdom in heaven.

Knowing how to read and interpret Scripture helps us to hear God's true message. As we begin to "go deeper" into God's Word, we can better discover the riches of his eternal truths.

One way in which we can gain new insights from Sacred Scripture is by praying with Scripture. *Lectio divina* ("divine reading") is one ancient form of prayer with Scripture. In this method, one attentively reads a passage of Scripture, meditates on the passage to see which word or words of the passage seem salient or personally meaningful in that moment, prays with the Scripture, and then contemplates the Word of God he or she has received. *Lectio divina* is a technique for reading Sacred Scripture not as an old book but as God's living Word, relevant to our own lives in today's world.

God's Word continues to speak to us. While the Gospel (the "Good News" of Christ) does not change, it is passed on by a living Church in which God plays an active role. We can come to know and hear God today through study of his living Word in Sacred Scripture and Sacred Tradition, which "make up a single sacred deposit of the Word of God" (*Dei Verbum*, 10).

LISTENING FOR GOD IN SACRED SCRIPTURE AND SACRED TRADITION

What is a favorite passage of Scripture for you? What do you hear God saying to you through this passage?

Look up in the *Catechism* a topic about which you have questions. Note how Scripture is used, both in the text and in the footnotes, to present the teaching of the Church in the context of Sacred Tradition. How does God speak to you through this integration of Sacred Scripture and Sacred Tradition?

Chapter 12
God Speaks to Us in Silence

In 1 Kings 19, the prophet Elijah is running for his life. He walks forty days and forty nights to the mountain of Horeb. He finds a cave, and takes shelter there. God tells him to go out and stand on the mountain, where the Lord will pass by. There, he experiences, in succession, a violent wind, an earthquake, and a fire, but Scripture tells us God was not in the wind, the earthquake, or the fire. Then Elijah hears "a light silent sound" (v. 12; some translations say, "a still, small voice"). At this, Elijah hides his face, for he knows that at last, the Lord is there. He had experienced multiple noisy, powerful events, but God himself was in the stillness, in the silence that followed.

Remember "the quiet game"? When I was a child, grown-ups were always suggesting we kids play the quiet game, especially if we were being noisy. We played the quiet game at school, in class at church, and in the car (especially on long trips). The game basically went like this: All the kids had to stop talking and be very still, careful not to make any noise. The first person to make a sound lost the game. Somewhere along the way, I realized that the quiet game was simply a ploy by the adults to get us to be quiet so they could have a reprieve from the kids. Also, we complained, the quiet game was *boring*. What could be fun about being still and quiet?

As kids, we are asked to be quiet so often that many of us develop an aversion to silence. If, like me, you come from a large, noisy family, you might feel as if you need some noise on in the background nearly all the time — television, music, something. Silence can be unnerving, at times, for many of us.

In my training as a psychologist, I remember hearing from one of my professors that the hardest skill to teach counseling students is not what to say, but when we should say nothing at all. "You have to learn to be comfortable with silence," he said, "because it's in the pauses that the client has time to think and reflect, to process." Not allowing this time, my professor contended, could prevent the client from gaining real insight in the therapy session. It could also keep the counselor from listening, because when we aren't comfortable with silence, we are often thinking about what we will say next, rather than reflecting on what we just heard. This has stuck with me, and I think it's made me a better therapist. I find that there are things I never have to say when I give clients an opportunity to sit in silence for a moment and come on their own to the insights I was going to offer.

We live in a noisy culture, one in which we are pressured to always be going, doing, saying something. All the noise around us can keep us from living in the present moment, because we offer ourselves no room to process the now, to reflect on the present. In the midst of this noise, God calls to us in Scripture: "Be still and know that I am God" (Ps 46:11). Saint Teresa of Calcutta spoke of the need to seek God in silence. "We need to find God," she wrote, "and he cannot be found in noise and restlessness. God is the friend of silence. See how nature — trees, flowers, grass — grows in silence; see the stars, the moon and the sun, how they move in silence. ...We need silence to be able to touch souls."* In his classic work, *The Imitation of Christ*, Thomas à Kempis wrote, "In silence and quiet the devout soul advances in virtue and learns the hidden truths of Scripture."†

Our ancestors in faith have given us a strong tradition of seeking God in silence. The Desert Fathers, who withdrew to the desert (primarily in Egypt) to pray in solitude, had a tremendous impact on Christianity in the third century. As more and more hermits withdrew to the desert, monastic communities started to form. These communities laid the foundation for monastic life in the centuries that followed. Great saints that came after them in subsequent centuries would look to the example of the Desert Fathers as they spent time in silence before God. This is particularly evident in the tradition of the contemplatives, who practiced a form of reflective prayer that Saint Gregory the Great called "resting in God."

At the heart of contemplative practices is the idea that we need to silence ourselves in order to allow the space for God to speak to us. Saint John of the Cross wrote, "It is best to learn to silence the faculties and to cause them to be still, so that God may speak."‡ Saint Faustina speaks of this in her *Diary* as well: "In order to hear the voice of God, one has to have silence in one's soul and to keep silence; not a gloomy silence but an interior silence; that is to say, recollection in God." She continues, "A talkative soul ... lacks both the essential virtues and intimacy with God. A deeper interior life, one of gentle peace and of that silence where the Lord dwells, is quite out of the question. A soul that has never tasted the sweetness of inner silence is a restless spirit which disturbs the silence of others."§

---

* Malcom Muggeridge, ed., *A Gift for God: Prayers and Meditations* (NY: HarperCollins, 2003), 83.
† Thomas À Kempis, *The Imitation of Christ*, Book I, Chapter 20.
‡ Saint John of the Cross, *Ascent of Mount Carmel*, 3:3.
§ Saint Faustina Diary, *Divine Mercy in My Soul*, par. 118.

Adoration of the Blessed Sacrament, silently contemplating and adoring the Real Presence of Jesus Christ in the Eucharist, housed in the tabernacle or monstrance, is an ancient form of prayer still practiced in the Catholic Church today. The *Catechism of the Catholic Church* explains the origin of Eucharistic adoration as follows: "The tabernacle was first intended for the reservation of the Eucharist in a worthy place so that it could be brought to the sick and those absent, outside of Mass. As faith in the real presence of Christ in his Eucharist deepened, the Church became conscious of the meaning of silent adoration of the Lord present under the Eucharistic species"(1379).

Saint John Baptiste Vianney, also known as the Curé d'Ars, lived in France in the late eighteenth and early nineteenth centuries. He struggled with his studies in the seminary but was allowed to be ordained due to his goodness. He became curé (or pastor) of the church in Ars in 1818, and much of his ministry was spent hearing confessions, as word traveled all over the country of his gift for administering the sacrament with great discernment and insight. Many people came from far away to go to confession with him, and toward the end of his life, he spent up to eighteen hours a day hearing confessions. Highlighting the value of spending time before God in adoration, the curé told about an older gentleman who, on a regular basis, spent many hours in the church, in adoration of the Blessed Sacrament. When Saint John asked the man what he was saying to God during these long visits, the man simply replied, "I say nothing to him. I look at him, and he looks at me."

In his Eucharistic meditations, Saint John reflected on this conversation, saying:

> When we are before the Blessed Sacrament, instead of looking about us, let us close our eyes and open our hearts. The good God will open

His. We will go to Him. He will come to us, the one to give, the other to receive.

It will be like a whisper from one to the other. What happiness do we not find when we forget ourselves to seek God? The saints forsook themselves in order to see God only, to work only for Him. They forgot all created objects to find Him alone. That is the way to heaven.⁵

If we want to be close, to truly be intimate with someone, the most important thing we can do is to spend time with them, and while spending time, to be fully present with them. Herein lies the treasure we find in contemplating Jesus in the Blessed Sacrament. He is really and truly present with us, and we are present with him. In such a circumstance, we couldn't help but draw closer to him. When Jesus walked the earth, his presence had the same effect. The Gospels are full of accounts of people of different ages and in various states of life who encountered Jesus, and after having spent time with him, were forever changed.

Saint John Paul II said the following about prayer: "There are several definitions of prayer. But most often it is called a talk, a conversation, a colloquy with God. Conversing with someone, not only do we speak, but we also listen. Prayer, therefore, is also listening."**

Spend time with Jesus. Look at him, and let him look at you. Let yourself slow down and rest in his presence. Let him speak to your heart in the silence. Listen to him, and see how you are changed.

---

⁵ Saint John Vianney, *Eucharistic Meditations of the Curé d'Ars* (Carmelite Publications, 1961), Meditation 22.

** Pope John Paul II, address to the Institut Catholique in Paris, June 1, 1980.

LISTENING FOR GOD IN SILENCE

When have you been in a quiet place and felt the presence of God? What did you hear God saying to you at that time?

Spend some time in a quiet place, perhaps before the tabernacle in the church, or at home before an icon. Acknowledge God's presence, and then spend some time listening to him. What might God be saying to you in the silence?

Chapter 13

God Speaks to Us in the Midst of Suffering and Struggle

One of the great privileges and most difficult parts of my work as a child psychologist has been the opportunity to accompany young people and their families through many different crises and struggles. From traumatic experiences, to grief and loss following the death of a loved one, to the pain of family separation, I have been called to walk with people who are suffering. Sometimes I feel painfully inadequate in this work. This is especially true when the age-old questions come up: Why does God allow suffering in the world? Where is God when I am struggling? There are no easy answers to these questions, and anyone who thinks there are probably hasn't yet had to suffer much. Still, we can count on the fact that suffering and struggle will come to each of us at some point in our lives. A quote often attributed to Saint Augustine says, "God had one son on earth without sin, but never one without suffering."

When asked about why people suffer, we might be tempted to offer slogans or easy answers, but the truth is, we don't fully understand why God allows suffering. Our faith teaches us that, on a macro level, suffering is caused by sin. In the creation story, Adam and Eve, our first parents, have everything they need, and creation is presented as working in perfect harmony until, in their desire to be like God, Adam and Eve do the one thing God commanded against. When sin and evil came into the world, we are taught, suffering followed. This doesn't, however, explain why individual people suffer, including those who are innocent and good, and it doesn't seem fair either that sometimes the wicked prosper. This problem is taken up in Scripture by the story of Job, a good man who loses nearly everything. Our ancestors in faith tended to believe that if we are good, good things will happen to us, and if we do bad things, we'll experience negative consequences. Even Jesus' own disciples were caught up in this way of thinking. They ask him, "Rabbi, who sinned, this man or his parents, that he was born blind?" (Jn 9:2). He tells them that neither the sin of the man nor his parents caused his blindness, and he heals the man "that the works of God might be made visible through him" (v. 3).

So where does that leave us on why suffering has to happen? We know that when suffering is caused by other people, it's often because they have misused the free will that God gives each one of us. God gives us the freedom to choose good or evil, not because it doesn't matter to him what we do, but because he wants us to do the right thing by choice. Sadly, people sometimes misuse the freedom they have to do good, and they do evil, hurting others in their path. And we often explain this by saying the person was "just evil." Still, it can be profoundly unsettling to see people make hurtful choices, especially ones that lead to suffering on a wide scale.

Sometimes painful and tragic things happen that seem to be nobody's fault. These are often the hardest to understand. Why do people get cancer and other serious illnesses? Why must there be earthquakes, floods, tornadoes, and hurricanes? Why doesn't God intervene when a terrible accident is about to happen? These questions are universal, I think, for people of faith. And any answers we are given often fail to satisfy when we are in the midst of suffering. But one thing we can know for sure is that *God is with us when we are hurting.* In the person of Jesus Christ, God entered into human experience, including human suffering. He endured torture and an unjust death at the hands of those who misunderstood or were threatened by his teaching. In Isaiah 53:3, the prophet Isaiah foretells "a man of suffering, knowing pain." Jesus knows what it means to be hurting. His human experience allows him to be in solidarity with us when we suffer. He is close to us when we are in pain. When we cry, he cries with us. So where is God when we are suffering? *He is right beside us.* In her diary, Saint Faustina writes, "It is you, Jesus, stretched out on the cross, who give me strength and are always close to the suffering soul."*

Not always, but sometimes, we might see signs of God's presence when we are suffering — God speaking to us in the midst of our pain. In an earlier chapter, I mentioned how I tried to teach the children I was working with at the residential treatment center for kids and teens to see the ever-present sparrows as signs that God had not forgotten them. God might also send us a message of care and support through other people — a caring word, a thoughtful gesture, right when we need it. "How did they know?" we might ask ourselves. Sometimes God speaks to

---

* Saint Faustina Diary, 1508.

us through a whole family or community.

I remember one particular family with two children, ages eight and ten, that came to be registered for religious education classes when I was the director of faith formation at a parish. The family had not attended church for years. I was glad to see them come back to the Faith, but the kids stopped coming to religious education sessions after a couple of weeks. I might have assumed that the family was just not that committed to their faith, and that their decision to return to the Church was short-lived. But something told me I needed to contact that family and find out what was going on. I called the mother and said, "Hi, we've missed the kids in class for the past couple of weeks. I just wanted to check in and make sure everything is OK." The mother began to cry. She said, "No, things are *not* OK." She went on to explain that her husband, the children's father, had abandoned the family in the middle of the night a couple of weeks before, and they had no idea where he was or if he was coming back. They were all understandably devastated, but in addition to their emotional distress, they had pressing practical needs. The father was the primary breadwinner in the family. They were struggling to buy groceries and pay the bills, and they were unsure if they would be able to keep the house they were living in.

I asked the mother if she could come up to the parish and talk with us in person. I gathered our pastor and the director of our ministry to families in need, and together we met with the family and worked out a plan to meet the immediate practical, emotional, and spiritual needs they were facing in this moment of crisis. Not only did the kids come back to religious education, but their mother became one of our best volunteers. She later said that the reason she became so involved at the parish was because in the moment her family was falling apart, the parish community was there for her. We became her family, and that made all the difference.

God might not will us to suffer, but he is able to bring good out of suffering. This is seen most clearly in Jesus' own death on the cross. The wickedest act ever committed — the murder of the Son of God — was used by God to redeem humanity and make us God's own daughters and sons. Saint Rose of Lima writes, "Our Lord and Savior lifted up his voice and said with incomparable majesty, 'Let all men know that grace comes after tribulation. Let them know that without the burden of afflictions it is impossible to reach the height of grace. Let them know that the gifts of grace increase as the struggles increase. Let men take care not to stray and be deceived. This is the only true stairway to paradise, and without the cross they can find no road to climb to heaven.'"†

Cradle Catholics might remember parents or grandparents telling them to "offer it up" when they were complaining about something. While it might be nice to get a little more sympathy, this phrase — "offer it up" — reflects a powerful truth, a truth that can give us strength in the midst of suffering. Because we are part of the Mystical Body of Christ, if we choose to, we can unite our sufferings with the sufferings of Jesus, putting our struggle at work for the salvation of the world. How is this possible? It's a mystery. But we see this teaching reflected in Scripture in the writings of Saint Paul, "Now I rejoice in my sufferings for your sake, and in my flesh I am filling up what is lacking in the afflictions of Christ on behalf of his body, which is the church" (Col 1:24). What, you might ask, is "lacking in the afflictions of Christ"? Certainly, Jesus' sacrifice is more than enough. But this passage points to a detail in God's design that gives meaning to our earthly suffering: God purposely left incomplete the work of reconciling humanity to himself in order to give us an opportunity to participate in that work with him. If we offer them to God, our sufferings are united to the sacrifice of Jesus, and in

† From the Liturgy of the Hours, optional second reading for the Feast of Saint Rose of Lima.

this way they take on the greatest meaning they could possibly have.

All this reminds me of some of the lessons I learned in my counseling training about helping people cope with suffering, either from grief due to a death or another type of loss. What is often most comforting to someone in the midst of struggle is not what we say, but our presence with them. After all, we all suffer through struggles and losses of some sort. Isn't it ironic that one of the few things we have in common seems to be the hardest for us to talk about? But our presence alongside a person who is suffering speaks something more profound than what we can say with words. It says that we are in this with them. Making the journey together, we can find meaning in the struggle. And this is what God does with us: He speaks to us through his solidarity with our suffering, through his presence with us in our pain. This allows us to make sense of suffering. And God can do something human beings often cannot — he can bring something good out of the struggle.

Does this mean that we should desire suffering, seek it, or even bring it upon ourselves? That would be a hard idea for me to swallow. (I don't know about you, but I don't like to suffer, and I have a hard time imagining that God likes to see his children suffer.) But perhaps we could all patiently bear just a little more annoyance in our daily lives, remembering what Jesus did for us. And when we face the inevitable periods of greater struggle that will occur (more for some of us than for others), we can lift that pain to God, be aware of how his presence speaks to us of his love, and offer our sufferings for the salvation of the world (including, yes, for those "poor souls in purgatory" they told you about when you were young). Doing so allows us to participate in the greatest work of Christ — to be swept up in his paschal mystery. And here's the thing about the paschal mystery — it doesn't end with Jesus' death. Our faith in Jesus teaches us that suffering and pain are never the end of the story for those who believe in him. Just as Jesus rose again from the grave, God promises those who are his disciples that a day is coming when he will wipe away every tear from our eyes (Rv 21:4). What a beautiful day that will be, when creation comes to its fullness, when we experience what it means to be fully in union with God and one another. The hardships we have endured along the way will make heaven even sweeter for us. Only our faith can help us to see suffering in this way.

LISTENING FOR GOD IN THE MIDST OF SUFFERING AND STRUGGLE

Reflect on the most difficult periods of your life so far. When have you experienced a sign of God's presence in the middle of a difficult situation? Sometimes we can see those signs more clearly in retrospect than we saw them at the time. What message was God speaking to you in the midst of your struggle?

Identify someone in your life who is struggling right now. How might you be a reminder of God's presence for them?

Epilogue
What Is God Saying to You?

In the preceding chapters, we have reflected on many different ways that God speaks to us in daily life. But the list presented in this book is by no means exhaustive. God also speaks to us powerfully in countless other ways. I like to think that God is always tapping us on the shoulder, patiently waiting to tell us what we need to hear. Jesus says, "Behold, I stand at the door and knock. If anyone hears my voice and opens the door, [then] I will enter his house and dine with him, and he with me" (Rv 3:20).

So how is God speaking to you right now? What is he trying to get across to you? If you're unsure, spend some time in prayer. Ask God to show you what he wants you to understand right now. Pray for the ability to hear his voice and the wisdom to discern it.

Is God offering you:

- reassurance of his love?
- help in making moral decisions?
- encouragement in your faith?
- direction for your life?
- reminders about virtues you need to work on?

Be open to what you might hear, even if it's surprising or unexpected — the life of discipleship is always an adventure. But it's a journey with a loving Father whom you can trust. Listen to him and, in the words of Our Lady at the wedding at Cana, "Do whatever he tells you" (Jn 2:5).

About the Author

Dr. Joseph White converted to the Catholic Faith while in graduate school at Virginia Commonwealth University, where he received a Ph.D. in Clinical Child Psychology. He later studied Catholic Theology at St. Mary's University in San Antonio. Dr. White is the Director of Catechetical Resources for Our Sunday Visitor Publishing and Curriculum and teaches courses in Catechetical Ministry at Holy Apostles College and Seminary. A frequent guest on Catholic radio and television, Dr. White has written eleven books and numerous articles about catechesis, Catholic education, and ministry. He is co-author of the *Allelu* and *Alive in Christ* religion series.